SINGLE-PARENT FAMILIES

SINGLE-PARENT FAMILIES

Richard Worth

Franklin Watts
New York   Chicago   London   Toronto   Sydney

Photographs copyright ©: The Bettmann Archive: pp. 1, 2;
New York Times Pictures/Barton Silverman: p. 3 top;
Randy Matusow: p. 3 bottom;
Miami Herald Publishing Company/Marice Cohn Band; p. 4 top;
Impact Visuals: pp. 4 bottom (Edward Peters), 5 (Evan Johnson), 7 top
(Katherine McGlynn); Reuters/Bettmann Newsphotos: p. 6 top;
Photo Researchers Inc./Susan Kuklin: p. 6 bottom;
Monkmeyer Press Photo/Mimi Forsyth: p. 7 bottom; Freda Leinwand: p. 8.

Library of Congress Cataloging-in-Publication Data

Worth, Richard.
Single-parent families / Richard Worth.
p.   cm.
Includes bibliographical references and index.
Summary: Discusses the reasons for, the needs, and the challenges
of single-parent families.
ISBN 0-531-11131-8
1. Single-parent family—United States—Juvenile literature.
[1. Single-parent family.]   I. Title.
HQ759.915.W67   1992
306.85′6—dc20   92-14230 CIP AC

Contents

SINGLE-PARENT FAMILIES

Introduction

This book looks at a relatively new phenomenon in America—the vast increase in the number of single-parent families. These are families created as a result of divorce or the death of a spouse or by a woman who becomes pregnant and gives birth without marrying the father of her child.

Single parenthood is largely a woman's role since the overwhelming majority of these families are headed by women. They must shoulder a variety of responsibilities that may include working and attending school, as well as running a household and raising children. What's more they must operate on their own for, unlike in the more conventional two-parent family, single parents usually can't depend on another parent to help with the children, or the rent, or the shopping, or the cleaning, or anything else. Single parents have an extremely difficult task which, they readily admit, often leaves them feeling exhausted at the end of every day. But, as you will see, they also talk about the exhilaration and sense of accomplishment they feel at handling so many things effectively.

What about the children in single-parent families? Single parents provide their children with love, security, and understanding. They instill their children with solid values, and prepare them for the complex world of adulthood, just like any two-parent family. But there is a difference—one parent can do only so much. A widow put it very well when she said that "children need that extra hug" which only two parents have time enough to give. The second parent also serves as an important role model of what it means to be a man or a woman, especially for adolescents struggling with their own identity. Finally, a fulfilling relationship between two parents provides an example for their children on which to pattern their own intimate relationships. As one boy, whose parents were divorced, explained: "I think I would be a good husband, but it would be a challenge because I never have really seen a truly good, solid home life. . . ."

Single-parent families, whether they result from divorce, death, or a woman's decision not to marry, face many of the same challenges. But each type of family also confronts many unique issues. In this book we will explore the varied facets of these single-parent families in an effort to understand how well they satisfy the needs of the adults and children who live in them.

PART ONE

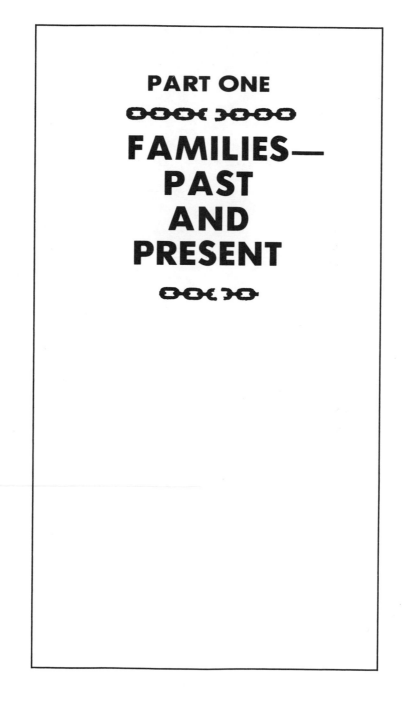

FAMILIES—
PAST
AND
PRESENT

1

The Rise of the Single-Parent Family

Single-parent families have always existed in America. For centuries, it was not uncommon for a woman to die in childbirth, leaving behind her husband to raise their family on his own. Or a man might die on the battlefield—as thousands did during the Revolution or the Civil War—and his widow and children might be forced to fend for themselves. Death was the primary cause of single-parent families, but there were other causes, as well. Some couples with children divorced, some parents abandoned their families, and some single women gave birth to illegitimate children. Even so, for the first three centuries of our history, there were very few single-parent families.

Not any more. Today there are over 10 million single-parent families (as compared to approximately 25 million families with two parents),[1] and the number of single-parent families is growing. Table I contains some statistics on families.

Why? The primary reasons are twofold: a rise in the divorce rate, and an increase in the number of children born to single women. To understand the causes of these developments, let's take a brief look at the history of the American family.

A PHOTO ALBUM

One of the most prized possessions of any American family is their photo album, frequently an oversized book stuffed with snapshots that record the family's history—weddings and graduations,

---

TABLE I
FAMILY VITAL STATISTICS

Two-parent families	25 million
Single-parent families	10 million
Divorces	1.2 million annually
Teenage pregnancies	1 million annually
Births to teenagers	500,000 annually
Children living with one parent	15.5 million (24% of total)
Percent of teenage mothers remaining single	$66\frac{2}{3}$
Percent of teenage girls reporting sexual experiences	53
Unmarried couples living together	2.8 million
Widows heading families	2.6 million

---

vacations and holiday celebrations, or simply family members posing together in front of the camera. Family photographs first became popular toward the middle of the nineteenth century when Samuel F.B. Morse, the developer of the telegraph, introduced photography into America from Europe, where it was invented. The families of that day sat stiffly for a photographer who tried to capture the strength and security which families symbolized to our ancestors. In one year, 1855, three million photographs were taken in New York City alone.[2] A few decades later, George Eastman invented the Kodak camera, and soon families began taking their own photographs and filling their own picture albums.

Some of these early photographs depicted family reunions—a huge gathering of uncles, aunts, grandparents, in-laws, and all of their assorted children. During the nineteenth century, family reunions became so popular that in the summer, communities would set aside a single week for them called "Old Home Week."[3] The occasion for these reunions might be the birthday of an aged parent, or an older couple's golden wedding anniversary. Old Home Week brought families together and, like the photo album, symbolized the enormous importance that Americans have attached to family values throughout our history.

LOOKING TO THE PAST

During the seventeenth and part of the eighteenth centuries, families were the most versatile institution in America. Most families lived on farms that were economically self-sufficient. They provided children with much of their education, arranged their play activities, instilled religious values, taught them farming, and cared for family members too poor or sick to care for themselves. In the colonial wilderness, families stayed together for survival, divorce was almost completely unavailable, and anyone who had committed adultery or gave birth to a child out of wedlock might be branded with an ''A.'' The colonists believed that the stability of society rested on the stability of the family.

Over time, however, the functions of the family began to change. Gradually people began to move into America's towns and cities, where the family was no longer self-sufficient. Adults who worked in trade or industry were expected to use their earnings to purchase food, clothing, and other items that their families needed. Many children no longer depended on their families to give them an education, but attended school. Instead of going to work on the family farm, they might apprentice to a craftsman who provided them with career training. Eventually, the primary role that parents began to play for children was to nurture them, socialize them in the ways of society, and then launch them into the adult world.

But the family played another critical role, too. Adults looked to it for emotional warmth, affection, and fulfillment. Throughout most of our history, men and women have not entered into marriages that were arranged for them—the custom in Europe—but they have arranged these marriages for themselves. This was in keeping with the new breath of freedom that blew across North America from almost its earliest days. As a result, adults hoped and expected to find happiness in their family relationships. In fact, as the other functions of the family slowly disappeared during the eighteenth and nineteenth centuries, happiness and psychological fulfillment became even more important to married couples.

Other changes also were occurring in the relationships between men and women. In the past, when a woman married she gave up all rights to any property she may have owned or any money she might earn during the marriage. Her husband owned everything. During the nineteenth century the laws changed, enabling women to retain control over their land and their earnings.[4]

Women began to see their roles differently, too. While most people still believed that the woman's place was in the home, many women were venturing outside it. During the nineteenth century, they joined the anti-slavery movement, led the temperance campaign against drinking, and attended women's rights conventions. Between 1890 and 1910, the number of women attending college tripled. More single women were working, and more wives were joining women's social groups where they could talk about their problems.[5] One of the things women were talking about more openly was sex, and more of them expected sexual fulfillment from their marriages.

The changing role of women, the expectation among more of them for sexual and emotional satisfaction, and their ability to keep control of their own property meant that they were less likely to suffer in an unhappy marriage. Meanwhile, the laws regarding divorce began to ease and divorces became somewhat easier to obtain. Men and women whose hopes for happiness and affection had been disappointed began divorcing in greater and greater numbers. Between 1870 and 1920, divorces increased fifteenfold, and by 1924 one in seven marriages ended in divorce court.[6] Although the majority of Americans continued to marry only once and to stay married for life, more and more people were clearly unwilling to remain in unhappy relationships.

DIVORCE AND THE SINGLE-PARENT FAMILY

Is not marriage an open question, when it is alleged, from the beginning of the world, that such as are in the institution wish to get out, and such as out wish to get in?

Ralph Waldo Emerson wrote these words more than one hundred years ago,[7] but he might just as easily have been speaking about our own era. While the vast majority of adult Americans marry and raise children, an ever increasing number continue to divorce. In fact, in 1991, one out of every two new marriages was likely to be dissolved.[8]

Several factors have contributed to the rising divorce rate. First, modern couples, far more than their parents and grandparents, enter a marriage expecting to find companionship, affection, and personal fulfillment. We live in an age that seems to put self-satisfaction ahead of the needs of others, and individuals who don't find satisfaction in a marriage or family relationship often decide to leave it. In the past, people endured unhappy marriages believing it was important to stay together for the sake of their children or the sake of the institution itself. This is no longer true for many couples.

Another factor contributing to the growing divorce rate is the changing role of women, primarily their entry into the workplace. Some percentage of women have always worked. Poor immigrant families, for example, were unable to survive unless every member, women and children included, worked together in the factories. Widowed and divorced women were also forced to work to support themselves and their families. But middle-class women, once they married, were expected to stay at home and care for their children.

Several events in the twentieth century changed this traditional role of women. During the Great Depression millions of men were laid off from their jobs and their families were threatened with starvation. To deal with this problem, women entered the labor market and took on menial jobs disdained by men. Women worked in factories and cleaned offices to earn a meager income. Although many men still believed that their wives should not work, they had little choice but to let them. During the depression, approximately twenty percent of white women and forty percent of black women held jobs.[9]

Another large increase in the number of working women occurred during World War II, when millions of men left their jobs to enter the armed forces. Women worked in aircraft facilities, ammunition plants, and shipyards. Fifty percent of these women were married.[10] They discovered a newfound sense of independence and self-sufficiency in these jobs, and they were reluctant to leave them when the soldiers returned home from the war.

But leave, they did. During the next decade and a half, women returned once again to the traditional roles of wife and mother. America entered a period which celebrated the value of "family to-getherness," symbolized by a home in the suburbs and a station wagon full of children driven by "the little woman."

Beneath the surface, however, women were often discontent because their lives as homemakers and mothers seemed boring and unfulfilling. Author Betty Friedan uncovered these feelings when she interviewed women for her book *The Feminine Mystique*, which was published in 1963. As Friedan so eloquently put it:

> *I have suggested that the real cause both of feminism and of women's frustrations was the emptiness of the housewife's role. . . . It is wrong for a woman, for whatever reason, to spend her days in work that is not moving as the world around her is moving, in work that does not use her creative energy. Women themselves are discovering that . . . they can have no peace until they begin to use their abilities.*[11]

Friedan's book helped ignite the women's movement, bringing women into the work force in much greater numbers than ever before. Women were now no longer dependent for survival on their husband's income. By emphasizing equality among the sexes, the women's movement also taught more wives to expect more understanding, cooperation, and sexual fulfillment from their husbands. If these elements were missing, women were far more likely to seek a divorce.

Meanwhile, divorces had become much easier for couples to obtain. State laws used to require individuals seeking a divorce, to prove that their spouses were guilty of an offense, like adultery, bigamy, or abandoning the family. Beginning in 1969, states began to grant "no-fault" divorces, which enabled couples to dissolve their marriages simply by claiming they were incompatible and unable to live together any longer.

Many of these divorces involved children. In 1991 approximately twenty-five percent of all children lived with a single parent,[12] usually their mother, who generally obtains custody of them in a divorce. Divorce is the major cause for the rise of the single-parent family in our society.

CHILDREN BORN TO SINGLE WOMEN

Contributing to the rise of the single-parent family is another significant development that has occurred during the twentieth century: An increasing number of single women are giving birth to children.

One of the primary reasons is America's changing attitudes toward sex. Throughout history, men and women have lived by a double standard. While men were permitted, even expected, to have sex before marriage, women were expected to be virgins. In fact "nice girls" were barely even allowed to kiss their fiancés before they announced their engagement.

During the twentieth century, these attitudes have changed. A survey conducted many years ago found that among women born prior to 1890, only ten percent had engaged in intercourse before they were married, while among those women born after 1910, almost seventy percent had had premarital sex.[13] As women entered the work force, they became more independent and far less willing to be bound by tradition. Nevertheless, most women still expected to be married, and although they may have engaged in sex before marriage, very few children were born out of wedlock.

Then, during the 1960s, our culture experienced a revolution in sexual morality. Once a taboo subject, sex was now discussed openly by couples seeking sexual fulfillment in their relationships—relationships that frequently did not involve marriage. For the first time our society began to permit a greater diversity in life-style. In 1991, approximately three million couples were living together without marriage.[14] A small but growing number of single women in their twenties, thirties, and even forties are choosing to bear children and raise them as single mothers. Some of these women become pregnant through artificial insemination, some adopt children, while others simply choose not to marry the fathers of their babies.

By far, the greatest impact of the sexual revolution, however, has occurred among young people in adolescence. Until the beginning of this century, the term adolescence did not even exist. Most children finished school after the eighth grade and soon afterward went to work on the family farm or in the factories. They generally remained at home under the watchful eye of their parents until they married and set up their own households, usually not too far away.

But, as jobs in business and industry became more specialized and complex, they required more education. After the turn of the century, parents gradually realized that their children needed to obtain at least a high school diploma if they wanted to succeed in the world, and an increasing number of young people were also going on to college. The period of adolescence had now been greatly enlarged; the number of adolescents was growing, and they were creating a distinct culture with its own clothes, its own language, and its own relationships. Adolescents began dating, then going steady; some even engaged in sexual intercourse. The automobile made it even easier for them to do all of these things away from the steady gaze of their parents. And the new sexual morality seemed to say premarital sex was acceptable.

According to the most recent surveys, over 50 percent of all teenage girls now report having sex[15] and many do not use birth control. The result is that one million teenage girls become pregnant each year, and more than one-half of them give birth to their children. This is four times the number of out-of-wedlock births in 1960. Perhaps the most startling statistic, however, is that while two-thirds of teenage mothers married during the 1970s, now two-thirds remain single.[16] Teenagers who head single-parent families exist in every American community—including white, black, Hispanic, and Asian—where they must confront unique problems that are often very difficult to solve.

DEATH AND THE SINGLE-PARENT FAMILY

A majority of single-parent families result from divorce or the decision by a single mother not to marry the father of her child. But there is also a third important factor contributing to the number of these families: the death of a spouse. The death may occur suddenly, or it may come after a long illness. No matter the cause, it creates enormous emotional scars for a single-parent family and places an additional burden on the parents and their children.

Of course, no one ever said that single-parent families have it easy. The people who live in them must face a special set of challenges. But along with them often go special satisfactions that are part of the everyday experience of being a single-parent family.

PART TWO

DIVORCE AND SINGLE-PARENT FAMILIES

2

Close-up:
Two Families

It seemed like a typical Saturday afternoon. Bill Matthews had taken his two children—Melissa, 12, and Bobby, 6—to a movie at the Twin Cinemas and then to Bobby's favorite fast-food restaurant. After they had settled into a booth in front of a large picture window and unwrapped their hamburgers, Bill decided it was finally time to talk about what had been on his mind all day.

"You probably realize that your mom and I haven't been getting along too well lately," Bill said. Bobby continued munching on his french fries, but Melissa stopped eating and just stared at her father as if she already knew what might be coming next.

Suddenly Bill hesitated, not sure whether to continue, whether he could really get the words out. "Your mother and I have decided—" He paused. Now Bobby began to fidget uncomfort-

Note: The stories in this chapter are fictional and the people are composites, developed from research and interviews.

ably in his seat, sensing that something was about to happen.

"—Your mother and I have decided not to live together. I'm going to be leaving tonight."

Bobby looked at his father. "You mean you're going away on a trip, Dad?"

"Don't you understand?" Melissa said sharply. "They're getting divorced."

Bill nodded. "I'm afraid so."

Suddenly, Bobby didn't feel hungry any longer. His eyes started to fill with tears.

"I know how you feel," Bill began.

"No you don't," Melissa broke in. "We were a family once, now we're not a family anymore."

Nearly fifty percent of all American children can expect to live with a single parent before they reach the age of eighteen.[1] Many of these single-parent families are created by divorce.

Most single-parent families (about ninety percent) created by divorce are headed by women. Nevertheless, over the past several decades, men have taken on a greater responsibility for child rearing. As a result, the number of men who receive custody of their children and raise them after a divorce has tripled, reaching approximately one million.[2] Table II has some statistics on divorce.

For each of these men and women and their children, divorce is a painful experience. And the changes they are forced to endure can be unusually difficult. But these families adjust, and many of them flourish.

A WOMAN AND HER FAMILY

Jim and Lisa met while they were still in college and married shortly after graduation. Neither of them had any idea how they were going to support themselves. But, fortunately, Jim had worked summers for a large food company that offered him a job in its management training program.

At almost the same time, a friend told Lisa that the local bank was looking for a computer programmer. Since she had earned her degree in computers, she had no trouble obtaining the position and stayed for five years—until the couple's first child, Jonathan, was born. Then Lisa decided to leave because she felt it was important to stay at home with him.

Unfortunately, Lisa found herself raising Jon-

TABLE II
FAMILIES OF DIVORCE: VITAL STATISTICS

Percent of families of divorce headed by women	90
Men receiving custody of children after divorce	1 million (10%)
Percent of men who fail to pay the required child support	30
Percent of homeless families headed by single parents	$66\frac{2}{3}$
Percent of children who rarely, if ever, see their fathers after a divorce	40
Percent of second marriages ending in divorce	60
Percent of children living in step-families by age 18	50

---

athan almost alone because Jim was never there to give her any help. He seemed to thrive on long hours at his office and seven-day work weeks. As his company promoted him, his travel schedule grew worse, and sometimes he would be gone as long as a month at a time to Europe or the Far East.

No sooner had Jonathan entered first grade, than Lisa became pregnant again with a second child—Kathy. Meanwhile, Jim continued his demanding schedule. And Lisa became something she said she never wanted to be—a nagging wife, criticizing Jim for neglecting her and leaving her alone to make every decision. Jim shot back that he would be happy to spend more time at home if Lisa would just get off his back.

The bickering between Jim and Lisa continued for three more years. And there were several violent blowups, with Jim even threatening to move out of the house. Finally after one terrible confrontation, he did leave and the couple decided to separate and obtain a divorce.

When Lisa told Jonathan about it, he said he was relieved because there wouldn't be any more arguments. But he missed his father and was afraid he'd never see him again. Kathy missed him too. She started complaining of stomachaches and told Lisa she didn't want to go to nursery school. And every night she'd crawl into bed and sleep beside Lisa so she could feel more secure.

Although Lisa tried to talk to Kathy and reassure her, she was feeling overwhelmed herself coping with all the responsibilities of being a single parent. The most pressing need was to find a full-time job because the alimony and child support that Jim had agreed to pay simply weren't going to be enough to take care of all the bills. While one family could survive on Jim's salary, he really couldn't run two households on it.

Financially, Lisa knew she'd be forced to make some serious adjustments. Jonathan, for instance, had been going to private school, but there was no way Lisa could afford to continue sending him. And both the kids would have to get along without any new clothes for a while.

By the end of the first year, Lisa also had to face another fact of life. She just couldn't afford to keep the house any longer.

This was the hardest realization of all. They'd lived there a long time, and all of Jonathan's closest friends were in the neighborhood. But he agreed to come along with Lisa when she went with the realtor to look at new houses, and eventually they found one—much smaller, but still adequate.

Throughout this period, Lisa realized that she was relying more and more on Jonathan to help her. Lisa needed him to be at home when Kathy got in from school because she was still at work. He'd fix Kathy a snack, start getting dinner ready and even put in a load of laundry. Lisa knew she was expecting more of Jonathan than any eleven-year-old should be asked to do—but there was no one else, she couldn't do everything herself.

Jonathan missed Jim terribly. Under the terms of the divorce, Jim had visitation rights (the right to see his children). He could have the children every other weekend and for several holidays. At first, he tried to see Jonathan and Kathy as often as he could. But as time went on, he began spending fewer and fewer weekends with them. He'd call and say he had to work or travel.

Then Jim's company transferred him across the

country and gradually he just lost contact with Jonathan and Kathy, except for a few telephone calls and presents at Christmas.

The child-support checks also began coming late, and some months not at all, so Lisa had an even more difficult time paying the bills. Fortunately, she received a promotion in her job, which helped a little.

The first year was really tough, but by the time it was over, Lisa realized she was going to survive. It certainly wasn't the same as having two parents to share all the responsibilities, or two paychecks to handle all the bills. But Lisa realized she could make decisions, and enjoy the satisfaction of accomplishing something on her own. She knew Kathy and Jonathan missed Jim and probably wished in some ways that everyone could have stayed together and worked out their problems. But they couldn't. Now they were a single-parent family.

A MAN AND HIS FAMILY

For Gail and Roger, twelve years of marriage ended suddenly when Gail announced that she had fallen in love with someone else and planned to move in with him. Roger felt rejected—he had lost his wife to another man. But when Gail told him she also wanted custody of their ten-year-old daughter, Carol, Roger drew the line: He wasn't intending to lose Carol, too.

Roger had a very close relationship with his daughter, much closer in fact than he had ever been able to maintain with Gail. He took great pride in following Carol's progress in school and felt extremely proud when she was named "Student of the Month." When she won the lead in her school play, Roger sat in the front row for both performances. He was also the coach of his daughter's soccer team which had reached the league semifinals, two years in a row.

It was difficult for Roger to accept the fact that he could easily lose this relationship if Gail obtained custody of their child, and he was reduced to seeing her only on weekends. So he decided to fight Gail, and after a long, bitter custody struggle, he finally won.

Unfortunately, the court battle that went on between her parents upset Carol terribly. She blamed herself for the divorce and believed her parents might have stayed together if only she had been a "good girl" and never misbehaved. Eventually Carol began having problems in school because she couldn't concentrate on her work, and her grades suffered.

For Carol, a large part of the problem was losing her mother. It wasn't that Carol didn't see her—Gail came every Saturday and took Carol to her new apartment across town. But Carol didn't like Joe—Gail's boyfriend—and still hoped her mother and father might somehow get back together. When Gail and Joe were married, Carol was very disappointed. And, a year later when they had a baby of their own, Carol felt completely left out and didn't want to visit her mother any longer.

Fortunately, Carol and her father had grown even closer. Nevertheless, Roger still had to admit that he was finding single-parenthood more of a challenge than he had ever imagined. Cooking was really the worst of it. Roger didn't have a clue about preparing even the simplest meal without burning something. So he found himself heating up frozen dinners, ordering pizza, or telephoning the nearby Chinese restaurant for their take-out specials. Although Carol never complained, dinners did become a little boring.

Roger also worried about leaving Carol at home alone after school, and he called every hour until he left work. He tried to spend more time with Carol, but his boss started complaining about the fact that Roger was letting some of his projects slip and not putting in enough hours on the job.

At times, Roger felt overwhelmed. He needed another adult in his life to talk over some of the problems that were on his mind and to help him deal with them. But how could he find this person? He had very little time during evenings or weekends after all the chores were done and Carol went to bed. And by that time, he was much too tired to talk anyway.

For now, he had Carol, and she would just have to be enough.

3

Families of Divorce

Sadness . . . anger . . . fear . . . guilt . . . relief . . . joy . . . accomplishment—these are some of the feelings experienced by single-parent families created through divorce. After her divorce from a man who was a compulsive gambler, one woman said:

> I had a sense of euphoria. It was a sense of freedom . . . of this tremendous weight being lifted off my shoulders. I was floating. I was so glad to be rid of this chain around my neck.[1]

Many adults have this immediate feeling of relief upon leaving an unhappy marriage. And some children are also relieved to see the marriage dissolve because it often puts an end to years of long-running arguments between their parents. Other children, however, react quite differently as Judith Wallerstein points out in her classic study of divorce, *Surviving the Breakup*. "Only a few children in our study thought their parents were happily married," Wallerstein explains. "Yet the overwhelming majority preferred the unhappy marriage to the divorce."[2]

Wallerstein found that young children were overcome with tremendous sadness. They wanted desperately to see the parent who had left home and worried that he or she might be lost to them forever. Older children, like the girl at the beginning of the last chapter, mourn because the family of their childhood—the traditional two-parent family—has been destroyed. Many single parents feel the same way, especially during the first year after the divorce. They have lost the American dream of a happy, two-parent family living in a white house surrounded by a picket fence. As one woman said:

> *I wanted the dream, and giving up the dream was devastating. . . . That summer I remember taking Mary (6 months old) to the lake, saying we got to get out of the house . . . we got to start doing normal people things. And (I remember) being there with all the mommies and daddies and children and having to leave before anyone saw me cry because it was just too painful to look at what all those people had, and I wanted and didn't have.*[3]

At first, it may be extremely difficult for single parents to cut through their sadness and fears and deal with the realities of running a family on their own. They may still look back nostalgically for what might have been and even blame themselves because they were unable to make the marriage work. One woman separated from her husband because she found their interests were incompatible. Although there was no anger or bitterness, the woman still felt guilty because she had put her son through the experience of seeing his father move out of their home. "In retrospect, I would probably never get divorced again," she admitted. "I would want to work things out, to fix them. I felt guilty. . . ."[4]

Sometimes children feel guilty, too, like ten-year-old Carol in the preceding chapter. As one boy recalled:

> *It was traumatic because . . . your whole family structure was totally disorganized in one fell swoop . . . you thought maybe you did something wrong . . . that maybe you were being too obnoxious, talking back too much to your parents, just doing too much of what a regular kid does.*[5]

Young children, especially, have an unrealistic view of their power to influence events. Not only can they feel that they caused the divorce, children may also imagine that by being "good" they can bring their parents back together. Instead of adjusting to their new, single-parent family, children wish for the old, familiar two-parent family again. It's a natural response to change.

At first, many children feel particularly vulnerable in their new families. Since one parent has already left them, they often worry excessively that the other parent may leave, too. Young children, in need of extra security, may want to sleep with the remaining parent. They may throw temper tantrums or complain of headaches and stomachaches to receive special attention. And they may even be reluctant to leave for school, fearing that when they return home, the remaining parent will have left them.

Some schools have established programs to help children cope with these problems. In several California schools, for example, students through eighth grade can participate in *Rainbows*, a support group which enables them to share their feelings about divorce. One child expressed the fear that her father, whom she sees only every other weekend, might die when he was away from her.[6] Another program, called *Banana Splits*, was launched in New York in 1978 and has since been adopted by schools in other states. At one meeting of *Banana Splits*, third and fourth graders met with a school psychologist and discussed their reactions following a divorce. Partway through the meeting, the psychologist held up a picture of a girl whose parents were pulling her braids in opposite directions. The psychologist asked how many children felt "torn apart" by their parents as a result of divorce, and all of them raised their hands.[7]

MONEY

Perhaps the most critical problem facing single-parent families is money. An income that supported one family before a divorce must now support two. And it may be inadequate.

As a result of many divorces, one parent, usually the father, is required to pay part of his income as child support to his former wife who has custody of their children. However, the child support may simply not be enough to pay for all of a family's expenses, such as rent, food, clothing, or any of the extras. In addition, approximately thirty percent of men fail to pay the child support they are required to provide.[8] Some just can't afford it. But far more often child support falls victim to the bitter conflict between a husband and wife that usually continues after their divorce. She may refuse to let him see his children unless he pays the child support, and he may refuse to pay her any support unless she grants him his visitation rights. Eventually, the father may drift away because it is too painful for him to deal with his former wife. He may stop visiting his children, and refuse to send the support checks.

In recent years, Congress has passed legislation which is designed to force parents to pay child support. If parents fall behind in their payments, employers can take money out of their paychecks. Some states have also issued "Most Wanted" lists of delinquent parents and arrested those who fail to pay child support. Nevertheless, many parents continue to violate the law. If a man changes jobs, for example, his new employer may not realize that he is required to pay child support and will not garnish his wages. Estimates are that only twenty percent of all delinquent parents are having money removed from their wages for child support.[9]

Since many women worked before they became single parents, they are able to survive on their own incomes. But just barely, and it often means changing their living standards. Single parents are frequently forced to sell their homes and move their families to lower-rent neighborhoods that they can afford (just as Lisa did in Chapter II). And moving can be very difficult for both parents and children. As one woman explained:

> One of the hardest things to do was to leave that house, because that was the last vestige of the dream, that house when I bought it, when we bought it, was everything I wanted for the rest of my life.[10]

Children may also regret moving, leaving behind a familiar house with all its memories, leaving their school and their friends for a new community and starting over again. They may also be forced to give up some of the luxuries that a two-parent family could afford, like summer camps, vacations, or new toys. And some young people even find that their college education is in doubt because their single parent can't afford to pay for it. Child support ends at age eighteen, and many divorced fathers refuse to pay college tuition.

These problems, however, seem minor by comparison to the daily struggle that confronts other single-parent families, who cannot survive financially. As Congresswoman Patricia Schroeder (D-Colorado) put it: "There are an incredible number of women who are one man away from poverty and don't know it."[11] Today fifty percent of America's poor families are headed by women.[12] Many of these families declined into poverty after a divorce occurred and the father refused to pay child support.

Marian's family is a typical example.* Marian had stopped working during her marriage to stay at home and raise her two children. After she and her husband divorced, Marian decided to look for a job. But without any recent work experience, she could only qualify for a position as a cashier at a local department store where the pay was extremely low. Somehow Marian and her children survived, at least until her former husband disappeared and his checks stopped arriving. Then the department store announced that it was closing and Marian lost her job. She fell behind in the rent

---

*Note: This is a composite family developed from research.

and was forced to sell some of her clothes and her furniture to buy food for herself and her children. Although Marian never imagined that she would ever have to live on welfare, she had little choice except to apply for it. This was the only way that her family could keep going.

The average income of single-parent families headed by women is less than fifty percent of that of all American families.[13] Many of these women are forced to apply for welfare, which includes monthly checks from Aid to Families with Dependent Children (AFDC) as well as food stamps, and Medicaid to pay for medical bills.

However, this meager income is often not enough to pay the high cost of food, clothes, and housing. In fact, an increasing number of single-parent families are being forced out of their homes to join the ranks of America's homeless. The United States Conference of Mayors reports that two-thirds of America's homeless families are headed by single parents, primarily women.[14] These families crowd into shelters for the homeless or the dingy rooms of welfare hotels, which are totally inadequate to house them. This creates enormous strains on parents and their children, bringing some families to the breaking point.

SINGLE PARENTS: JUGGLING CHILDREN AND WORK

During the first year following a divorce, the stresses and strains on single parents may seem too much, especially as they try to handle the dual responsibilities of work and child-rearing.

Many single parents report feeling overwhelmed, like Lisa in the earlier pages of this book. A single father explained that he frequently had night meetings at his job. He would leave work at 4:30 to be home when his son, aged twelve, arrived from school. Then he would cook dinner, eat with his son, and leave him doing his homework while he went out for a meeting. "That was exhausting,"[15] he said.

A single mother who was holding down a full-time job and raising a young child said she felt guilty for not being able to spend more time with her daughter:

> From the time I picked her up at day care until the time she went to bed, . . . that was our time and it was sacred and invaluable . . . Even so, there was guilt. I knew that quality time was important and that's what I tried to focus on, but I felt that I was trying to justify the fact that I didn't have more time for her. I remember one day she was in her room playing with her doll saying, "Not now, Mommy has to work," and thinking about what she was learning from what I was teaching her. . . .[16]

Of course, this same problem arises in a two-parent family where both parents work. However, children often feel that they receive more attention when both their mother and father are living with them. Even if a father continues to visit his children after a divorce, they may still feel angry that their parents couldn't work out their differences. As one teenager put it:

> It's not the home life that you really expected. You know, you expected a home life that your parents are married and . . . it's not normal at all . . . you have friends who have normal family lives and you always wonder why you couldn't have the same thing.[17]

Some children take out their resentment on the single parent. As a result, the relationship between parents and children may grow worse during the first year after the divorce. Other children, however, seem to grow closer to their single parent. They willingly undertake additional responsibilities, like cooking, cleaning, and caring for younger siblings to help their parents who are trying to hold full-time jobs while coping single-handedly with all the problems of running a family. A single parent may even begin to rely on the child as a confidante, someone with whom to share the sorrows and frustrations as well as the joys and accomplishments that occur in the aftermath of a divorce.

PARENT–CHILD RELATIONSHIPS

For a parent alone, a child can easily take the place of another adult. Many single parents report that they are too tired by the end of the day to even think about looking for the companionship of other adults. Instead, they turn to their children. If the support check is late, or the boss is too demanding, they complain to their children. If they want to go to the movies or out to dinner with someone, they ask their children. At first, a child may feel flattered to assume this new role and enjoy the greater sense of importance it brings. But this so-called parent-as-pal relationship can create serious problems.[18]

A child may feel anxious and uncomfortable with this unusual situation, but afraid to tell his or her parent for fear that she might get angry and even leave. Children might also feel guilty about going out with their friends and leaving parents alone at home. Some children may even begin rebelling against their parents. And a parent who has acted like a pal with her children may be incapable of disciplining a child who needs it.[19]

However, many single parents avoid these problems by turning to other adults (especially family members) and developing new friendships and new interests after their divorce. One single father explained that his mother helps him care for his son, giving him the opportunity to occasionally go away on weekends. A single woman said that she also relied on her family for support:

> My biggest support system was my sister and my mother. I had other adults that I could talk to and I had good relationships with them plus, interestingly enough, I had and still have a very good relationship with my mother-in-law. She would help me take care of the baby. We would go shopping together and we'd talk on the phone.[20]

Many adults seem to possess the inner resources to be strong, capable single parents, and they also seem to enjoy the responsibility. As one single father put it: "It's wonderful in many ways being able to make decisions by myself and not having to waste a lot of energy coming to some kind of common agreement (with my former wife)."[21] A single mother talks about her feeling of confidence:

> I learned that in a pinch, the only one you can ever really count on is yourself. I've been through some pretty tight pinches and came through okay. So I trust me. And that has given me a sense of confidence.[22]

Psychologists point out that in successful single-parent families children often grow up with a very positive role model of a self-confident woman who is capable of doing many things on her own. Children also have more responsibilities, and unlike their peers in many two-parent families, they know how to cook and clean.[23] Much of what happens in a single-parent family depends on the relationship between the parent and the child, just as it does in any family.

4

The Long-Term Effects of Divorce

Dr. Judith Wallerstein has studied single-parent families five years and ten years after a divorce. She has discovered that the most important factors in a child's development are the attitude of the single parent (usually a mother) and the quality of her parenting.[1] Wallerstein found that many women, especially those in their twenties and early thirties, saw the divorce as a second chance in life, an opportunity to put the past behind them and make up for the mistakes they had made in their marriage. They found jobs, established satisfying new relationships, and threw themselves into the responsibilities of raising their children.[2] Juggling these tasks was never easy. But as time went on, women developed more confidence in their ability to handle all of them, their self-esteem grew, and they created a secure, loving home environment for their kids.

Some women, however, were not so successful. Wallerstein's interviews with them revealed that five years and ten years after their divorce they were still experiencing serious problems. Women over forty, who had been married longer, found it far more difficult to put their marriage in the past and begin a new life. They missed their role as a wife and a marriage partner in a two-parent family. And, unlike the younger women, they had far less chance of finding new partners because of their age. These women often suffered from severe loneliness, depression, and feelings of disappointment at what their lives might have been. They also suffered financially, seeing their incomes decline after the divorce at the very time that their former husbands seemed to be advancing in careers and increasing their incomes.[3] This only fueled the anger and bitterness these women felt toward their ex-spouses.

Children can easily become caught up in this conflict, taking one parent's side against the other. They may resent the fact that they and their mother must struggle financially while their father seems to have so much more money. Some parents use their children as weapons in the battle against each other. Unfortunately, these conflicts only increase a child's feelings of insecurity and unhappiness. Studies have found that one of the most important factors in the adjustment of children following a divorce is the relationship between their parents. Somehow, parents have to put their own disagreements aside for the sake of their children. It's not easy because divorce creates tremendous bitterness and resentment. But if these feelings spill over into the parents' relationships with their children, it is the children who suffer most.

One relationship is often destroyed as a result of divorce—the bond between a child and the parent who moves out.

A recent survey indicates that over forty percent of the children in families of divorce rarely, if ever, see their fathers.[4] (See Table II in Chapter 2.) Some fathers didn't spend much time with their children during the marriages so it is perhaps quite natural that they would drift away after the divorce. Others feel guilty about causing the divorce and the pain it may have inflicted on their children, so they visit infrequently and eventually not at all. For others, the entire visiting process is simply too emotional—having their children again for short periods of time, and then losing them creates too much sadness. Many fathers also feel resigned that they will be replaced in their children's hearts when their mothers remarry.

But these fathers are often wrong. They are not replaced. As one out-of-home father explained:

> I believe children don't want to lose you. You don't know that at the time, but they are panicked that they might lose you. So you have a window that's open, I believe, for the first year that if you show them you love them and if you show them that you're going to be there regularly they're going to somehow or other overcome their Mom [even if she] is giving them a hard time to see you 'cause they really don't want to lose you.[5]

Wallerstein's studies confirm this statement. In fact, she points out that one of the key factors in a child's adjustment in the years following a divorce is his or her relationship with the visiting parent, who is usually the father.[6]

Many fathers, understandably, have a difficult time playing the role of visiting father because there are no clear guidelines on what to do or how to stay involved with children whom they don't see every day. Bob is one divorced father who has remained involved. He explains that men must make the same commitment to their children that they do to their careers. As men advance in a career, they may be transferred to other parts of the country and easily lose touch with children whom they see only occasionally. However, Bob gave up a career opportunity just to stay near his children.

You had those children. You are responsible for them. You have fifty percent, if not more, responsibility for their upbringing and their success, hopefully, and their life. You have no right to abandon them. . . .[7]

Bob has his children with him every other weekend and for breakfast on alternate weeks. Since both children are several years apart, he has each one separately for dinner and an overnight so he can give them individual attention. Children who have only limited amounts of time with an out-of-home parent often resent sharing all of it with their siblings and they appreciate time alone with their parents.

The impact of this involvement on a child can be enormous. Wallerstein found that boys suffer a loss of self-confidence and self-esteem when they lose a meaningful relationship with their fathers. The result may be lower achievement in school, less ambition, more aggressive behavior towards their peers, and very limited goals for the future. This finding is confirmed by another study that shows that the longer boys are without their fathers the fewer grades they finish in school.[8] Fathers provide their sons with important male role models to help them define who they are and who they want to become.

Bob explained that he developed a close bonding with his teenage son through sports. "We are both baseball freaks," he said. But the relationship didn't end here. Bob remained involved in every aspect of his son's life. He knew his teachers, his coaches, and his friends. He continued to live nearby his son to make visiting as easy as possible. For as young people enter adolescence, they often find that a weekend with an out-of-home parent who lives in another community or another state takes them away from activities with their friends. Bob's son could easily invite friends over to his father's house which worked out well for everyone. As time went by, the bond between Bob and his son remained so close that the boy eventually decided to leave his mother's home and live with his father, who is now his single parent. As the boy explained:

> My father's become a mother and a father and I think anybody could really do that if they put their mind to it. . . . You know, he cooks dinner . . . he does laundry, he cleans . . . he goes to my games, he talks to me about sports, he talks about girls. You know, he's always there, he's doing everything one hundred percent instead of just doing fifty percent.[9]

As children, girls often seem to adjust to a divorce more easily than boys. They can express their feelings more openly, and they often turn to friends for support.[10] Nevertheless, the effects of the divorce frequently do not disappear. Some girls suffer from a poor self-image, just like their brothers. They remain angry at their parents years afterward for not resolving their problems and preventing the breakup. They also feel rejected by fathers who have left and fail to visit them. Even fathers who do visit may appear so infrequently or irregularly that they cannot maintain fulfilling relationships with their daughters. For some men, emotional closeness seems impossible. One single mother explained that her daughter was feeling

> *a lot of pain over the fact that when she was with [her father] she wasn't with him because he was emotionally not there. He would either have friends over or even a girlfriend over or they would go to visit other people. She had no home time with him or if they were home, at his home, he'd be watching a football game and not allow her to speak to him. He was just emotionally unavailable to her.*[11]

This girl's experience simply reemphasizes the importance of a quality relationship between an out-of-home father and his children.

As girls enter adolescence and adulthood, the divorce can create another problem for them. They may be reluctant to develop close male/female relationships, fearful that they will end the same way as their parents' marriage. While young women may look forward hopefully to a successful marriage, they're also afraid of failure, afraid of being rejected, just as their mothers were by a man who walked out on them. And these feelings may only be reinforced if their father remarries. As a result, many girls may need the special help of a counselor or other professional to develop a healthy attitude about their own sexuality and their relationships with boys. Although the majority of young women and men from divorced families will eventually marry—and many of them successfully—the memory of the divorce may never disappear.

JOINT CUSTODY

In the vast majority of divorces, one parent (usually the mother) receives sole custody of the children. However, some parents believe that they can reduce the negative effects of divorce on their children through an arrangement called joint custody. Under joint custody, parents decide to share responsibility for all the major decisions affecting the children—health care, schooling, etc. And in some joint custody arrangements children also divide their time almost equally between each parent, which usually means that parents must live near each other. Children may spend part of every week with each parent, for example, or alternate weeks between their mother and father. In a sense, then, children have two single parents.

These arrangements require enormous cooperation between both parents. They must be able to set aside the conflicts between themselves and give top priority to their children's well-being. The key seems to be flexibility. Parents need to accept the fact that rules may be different in each household. For example, a father may permit his children to watch more television or stay up later than their mother allows. Standards of neatness and cleanliness may differ, too.

Effective communication is also essential—a very difficult task for parents who could not get along with each other in a marriage. Parents must talk with each other constantly so each one is completely aware of the child's needs. Is the child suffering from any physical illness? What are his or her homework assignments and when must they be completed? Who are the child's friends and what activities do they have planned together?

Flexibility and communication are important not only for parents, but for children, too. They must be able to move easily back and forth between households that may be entirely different. Some children have difficulty leaving one parent to live with the other, and a few days later repeating the process all over again.[12] Others resent the need to have two rooms or two sets of clothing. However, some children do report that they feel less impact from the divorce because they can maintain their relationship with each parent.[13]

Once again the quality of the parenting by both parents is the most essential factor in each child's sense of well-being. This is critically important whether the child lives in a joint custody or sole custody arrangement.

NEW RELATIONSHIPS

Like all families, the single-parent family experiences significant changes as children grow, or parents undertake new jobs, or the family moves to a different neighborhood. One of the most far-reaching changes, however, is the new sexual relationships that parents develop with adults outside the family. For many children, the whole idea that their parents are sexual beings comes as quite a revelation. Among adolescents, who are just beginning to date and understand their own sexuality, the fact that their parents are also dating and involved in intimate relationships may be difficult to accept. Adolescents need parents to act like parents. And parents are not expected to date because this makes them seem like adolescents.

Young people may also have mixed feelings about a new adult entering the family. The close bond between a parent and child often weakens as the parent develops an intimate relationship with another adult. While a parent needs this relationship, children often feel as if they have suddenly taken second place, no longer as important as they were before. A natural reaction for many children is to feel angry and jealous, at least at first, until they begin to accept the relationship.

Children also wonder what role this new person may eventually play in their family. Will their mother's date someday become their stepfather? Will he try to replace their real father? Does he have children who will become their stepbrothers or stepsisters? How will these changes affect their role in the family and their relationship with Mom?

Single parents generally try to be sensitive to their children's concerns. As a single mother finds herself falling in love with a man, she usually wants to know how her children feel about him. She watches to see how they interact with him and what kind of stepfather he is likely to be. These factors play an important role in her decisions about the future.

Eventually, the majority of single parents remarry. Then, the single-parent family becomes a two-parent family again.

PART THREE

TEENAGE
SINGLE
MOTHERS

5

Close-up:
A Mother and Child

Last year, over one million teenagers became pregnant. Some of these young women received an abortion, others had a miscarriage. But approximately one-half gave birth to children.[1] Twenty years ago, two-thirds of these teenage mothers were married. Today the majority are unmarried and never marry the fathers of their children.[2] Instead they raise them in a single-parent family.

Helen is one of these teenagers. When Helen was sixteen, she began going out with Ray, who had dropped out of high school a few years earlier and now worked in the local video store. Helen's parents were not happy about this relationship and tried to prevent it, but to no avail. Helen would simply tell her parents that she was visiting a girlfriend, and instead she'd wait for Ray at the store

Note: The story in this chapter is fictional, and the people are composites developed from interviews and research.

until he finished work and they'd spend the evening together at his apartment.

Helen had attended sex education classes in school and knew how to prevent pregnancy. But she was afraid to talk to her mother about the pill or admit that she was planning to have sex. Somehow, Helen believed that she could avoid becoming pregnant—she'd just be luckier than a couple of the other girls she knew who had dropped out of high school. And if she wasn't, well, that might not be so bad, either. Living at home was growing harder for her every day. Helen's mother was always criticizing her for something. She also seemed to pick on her father whenever he walked through the door. About six months earlier, Helen's dad had lost his job and so far he hadn't found another one. Since then, her parents seemed to argue about money almost constantly. If she became pregnant, Helen thought, she could move in with Ray or even marry him. Then she'd have two people to love her, and she'd be out of her house forever.

When Helen missed her menstrual period two months in a row, it appeared that her plans for the future were taking shape a little sooner than she had expected. At first, Helen refused to admit that she was pregnant. But she couldn't hide her morning sickness from the watchful eye of her mother, or the fact that she was putting on weight. When her mother finally confronted Helen, she broke down and admitted it. Her mother was devastated. She had hoped Helen would finish high school and even attend college. Now those things seemed impossible.

Helen expected her mother to be upset, but she was totally unprepared for Ray's reactions. When she first told him, he seemed pretty relaxed about the pregnancy. But inside Ray was frightened. A few days later he called Helen and asked her to consider an abortion. He even offered to pay for it. Helen was stunned and disappointed. She told Ray she planned to keep the baby and pleaded with him to help her. But he refused. Soon he was making excuses for not seeing her, and eventually he simply drifted away.

Meanwhile Helen's parents gradually began to adjust to the idea of becoming grandparents. On Thursday evenings after she finished work, Helen's mom went with her to childbirth classes at the local clinic. And since Helen's dad had finally found himself a new job, he could afford to buy a few extra things for the baby. Nevertheless, both of them still had mixed feelings about the changes that a new child would bring into their lives. They thought their days of parenting were almost over, and they were not really looking forward to beginning again.

Once the baby arrived, the family's entire routine changed dramatically. Although Helen loved her little boy, she wasn't ready for the enormous responsibility involved in caring for him. After all, Helen was a teenager accustomed to going out with her friends whenever she wanted. Suddenly, she found herself completely tied down with a baby—a little boy who had to be fed and bathed and clothed, a little boy who had to be looked after almost constantly.

At first, Helen's mother stayed home from work to help her adjust to the routine. (And she even got up in the middle of the night when the baby cried.) But mostly he was Helen's responsibility. While her friends went to school, enjoyed their usual activities, and made their plans for the future, Helen stayed at home with the baby. Her mother agreed to babysit several nights a week so Helen could take special classes and eventually finish high school. She didn't intend to drop out because she knew what that could mean for her. But when weekends arrived and Helen wanted to be with her friends, her mother drew the line.

"You should have thought of that before you became pregnant," she said.

Gradually, the conflicts between them began to grow. Helen felt that her mother was constantly interfering and telling her how to raise the baby. She criticized Helen for spending too much time on the telephone and not watching the child. She would call the pediatrician and check up on Helen to make sure she was following his advice. They clashed over what the baby was wearing, whether he was clean enough, and whether he was eating properly.

One night after an unusually bitter argument, Helen packed up all the things she needed for herself and the baby and moved in with one of the girls she had met in her class. Helen figured she could apply for welfare and receive enough to live on her own. Other girls did, and they seemed to do just fine without any advice from Mom. But this decision proved far more difficult than Helen had ever imagined. Welfare provided only a meager income, far less than she needed to pay for day care. So she had to drop out of school. Since Helen's girlfriend was rarely at home, she spent most of her time alone except for the baby. And she promptly discovered that one thing was even worse than arguing with her mother—loneliness.

Fortunately, Helen and her mom had never lost contact. One day she called her mother and asked if she could return home. At first, it was difficult for Helen to get used to the fact that she had to live under her parents' roof again. But she missed her mother and needed her support, and eventually they were able to settle their differences and improve their relationship.

6

Children Having Children

Helen's story illustrates many of the questions surrounding any girl who becomes a young, single parent. Why does the pregnancy occur? What role will the father play? How will a girl's parents react? Why should a girl remain in school after the birth of her baby? How will her life change when she becomes a parent? What will be her relationship with her own parents? How will they resolve the responsibilities of caring for a child? What role will welfare play in the life of a young mother? Let's begin looking at some of the answers.

WHY PREGNANCIES OCCUR

America has the highest rate of teenage pregnancy in the industrial world. It is more than twice as high as that in England and Canada, for example, and over three times the rate in Sweden.[1] About sixty percent of these pregnancies occur among white teenagers, although the fertility rate (pregnancies per number of girls) is much higher among black teens.[2] Table III contains some statistics on teens and pregnancy.

Why is teenage pregnancy so much more common in the United States? One reason seems to be our attitudes toward sex and birth control. In Europe, for instance, birth control is prominently advertised on billboards and in magazines. While European parents may not like the fact that their teenage children are having sexual relationships, they are far more concerned about the possible consequences and want to make sure their sons

TABLE III SINGLE AND PREGNANT VITAL STATISTICS	
Percent of children born to single women	22
Pregnancy rate among U.S. teenagers, ages 15–19	95 per 1,000
Percent of teens who fail to get medical care in first trimester	51
Percent who fail to get medical care until last trimester	10
Percent of teenagers who don't finish high school after birth of baby	50
Percent of teenagers who have more than one pregnancy	$33\frac{1}{3}$
Percent of schools providing sex education	93

and daughters use birth control to prevent pregnancies. In the United States, by contrast, many parents want to stop their children from having sex and often won't even discuss the issue of birth control. The message to teenagers is clear: Sex is immoral and should never be planned, so we should never use birth control because that would be admitting that we are planning to have sexual relations.[3]

Although sex education is widely taught in United States schools, many teenagers profess ignorance when it comes to understanding how pregnancy occurs. Some girls also report that they're afraid of using birth control measures, such as the pill, because of the possible side effects. What's more, health clinics often refuse to dispense pills without parental consent, which involves embarrassing conversations between teenagers and their parents. There is a general attitude that if teenagers have birth control devices, they will be more likely to engage in sexual relations. Although this attitude is unsubstantiated by any studies, it frequently prevents parents and teenagers from rationally discussing the issues of sex and birth control. In addition, girls generally seem reluctant to talk to their boyfriends about using some form of protection. As a result, a recent study reveals that over eighty percent of all pregnancies among American teenagers are unplanned.[4]

Evidence suggests, however, that this figure may be an overestimate. In a series of articles that first appeared in *The Washington Post*, reporter Leon Dash describes his conversations with single teenage mothers and their families living in Washington, D.C., who are in the lower socioeconomic class. As Dash explains, not one of these girls be-

In the nineteenth century, as they do in the present, families posed for portraits. In the past, however, two-parent families, such as the one shown, were the rule.

Above: In the past, not only did families stay together at home, but they often worked together as well.

Below: During World War II, large numbers of women— fifty percent of them married—worked in defense industries, contributing to women's growing sense of independence.

Above: Children often feel torn when parents split up, as is shown in this picture used in a special program for children from broken homes.

Below: The living conditions of some single-parent families are not always the most glamorous, but family closeness can persist nonetheless.

*Above: This single mother of five is
twenty-two years old and was staying in a women's
shelter at the time the photograph was taken.*

*Below: Unfortunately, single parenthood drives many
families into homelessness. This family is living
in a shelter in New Jersey.*

*These teen mothers are enrolled in a special
high school program for young parents.*

Birth control is much more openly practiced in Europe than in the United States, which still has a double standard about sex. It is frequently portrayed on TV, in movies, and in commercials, but a puritanical attitude exists about discussing and teaching birth control. Here a couple purchases a condom from a machine installed in a French nightclub.

Mom, seventeen, poses with her baby and mother. Just when she was looking forward to perhaps moving beyond her own role of mother, Grandma often finds herself once again changing diapers, baby sitting, and having her energies consumed by a young child.

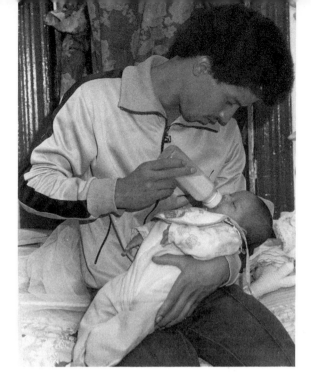

*Above: This seventeen-year-old father is feeding his
daughter at his girlfriend's house. He may
not have a job, but he has not abandoned
his child as many men do when times are tough.*

*Below: Death can create a single-parent family, which
shares many of the same problems found among single-
parent families created by other causes.*

*A single mother and her four children taking
a stroll near New York's Central Park.*

came pregnant by accident. All of them wanted a baby. One girl put it this way:

> *When girls get pregnant, it's either because they want something to hold on to that they can call their own or because of the circumstances at home. Because their mother doesn't pamper them the way they want to be pampered or they really don't have anyone to go to or talk to or call their own. Some of them do it because they resent their parents.*[5]

These same motives apply to many teenage girls who become pregnant and have a baby, no matter what their background is or where they live. A teenager may see a child as someone to love and help her make up for an unhappy home life where no one seems to care about her. Or she may become pregnant to strike back at her parents who are always criticizing her. In some cases, she may even hope that the father of the child will agree to marry her so she can leave home and they can set up their own household. Sometimes marriages do occur, but the divorce rate among teen couples is even higher than the national average for adults.

During his interview with the teenage girls in Washington D.C., Dash found that several other motives for pregnancy kept appearing over and over. For these girls, pregnancy served as a rite of passage into adulthood. One girl told Dash she was afraid of being infertile and wanted a baby to prove that she was capable of bearing children. Others explained that their friends had become pregnant and they felt peer pressure to follow. For boys, the pregnancy was often a status symbol—a macho badge of honor. Dash's interviews also revealed that several boys felt pressure from their girlfriends, who wanted to become pregnant.[6]

For these teenagers, there seems to be no reason to postpone pregnancy because they grow up in poverty and have little or no hope for the future. Unlike middle-class young people who often plan to go on to college and enter successful careers, the children of poverty are not usually given these same opportunities. The role model for a teenage girl is not a college graduate or a successful career woman, but her own mother or grandmother, whose life has usually been spent holding down low-paying jobs and raising her own children.

Today, the majority of these women head single-parent families. And ninety percent of their teenage daughters who become pregnant will follow in their footsteps.[7] Why don't these girls marry the father of their children? A primary reason is that the father is usually unemployed or is underemployed at a menial job. Nevertheless, some of these young men still try to help their girlfriends financially after they become pregnant. Many others, however, simply drop out of the picture—too overwhelmed by the burdens of parenthood, or simply uninterested in being a parent, or just unable to act like a father because they never had a real father themselves.

Some experts believe that another reason why pregnant teenagers remain single is the welfare system. If a girl's income falls below a certain level, she can qualify for money from Aid to Families With Dependent Children as well as food stamps and Medicaid. However, several of the women interviewed by Leon Dash explained that they disliked welfare because it was so humiliating. Welfare assistance was also completely inadequate to support themselves or their children; and they were relieved, they said, to stop accepting it as soon as they could find jobs.[8]

Studies have shown that while welfare provides teenage girls with a safety net, it is not a primary reason why they choose to have their babies and remain single. They simply see no acceptable alternative.

THE INITIAL REACTIONS
TO PREGNANCY

Pregnancy changes a teenage girl's entire life. For some, it is a welcome event, one that they've hoped for and planned. But for many other girls, the pregnancy comes as a complete surprise, a frightening miscalculation. They may feel ashamed and even try to deny the pregnancy to themselves, their friends, and above all, to their parents.

Eventually, of course, their parents usually do find out. As you recall, Helen's mother was initially disappointed in her daughter. She had high expectations for Helen's future but realized that with the pregnancy, many of them might never be fulfilled. Helen's parents also resented the idea of becoming grandparents and helping her care for a baby after assuming that their days of child rearing were finally over.

Some parents feel very angry at their daughters for becoming pregnant, and accuse them of being promiscuous or betraying their parents' trust. "After all I've done for you," a father might say, "look how you pay me back." While this father heaps blame on his daughter, other parents blame themselves for what occurred and feel that they have failed to raise their daughter properly.

DEALING WITH THE PREGNANCY

Once these initial reactions have been expressed, parents and children must then begin the difficult task of actually dealing with the pregnancy. For many girls, abortion will be the solution, but others will choose to continue with the pregnancy and have their baby.

For these girls one of the most important issues is proper health care during the pregnancy. Sadly, recent studies reveal that more than half of all pregnant teenagers do not see a doctor during the first three months of their pregnancy.[9] Often, it's because these girls try to deny their pregnancy and hope that it will miraculously disappear. In some cases, adequate health care may not be easily available or affordable. A full ten percent of all pregnant teenagers receive no care until the final trimester.[10]

While teenagers are fully as capable of having healthy babies as older women, they must receive periodic examinations, maintain a nutritious diet, and avoid alcohol, tobacco, and drugs, all of which can harm the growth of a fetus inside their womb. However, too many teenagers fail to follow these guidelines. Their babies are more likely to be born premature or to have a low birthweight. And low birthweight babies have a higher rate of death, they suffer from more illness during infancy, and they grow up with greater learning and behavior problems.[11]

A healthy pregnancy is critical for the future of both the mother and her child. This requires cooperation between a teenager and her parents, a willingness to accept what has happened, to deal with it realistically, and to prepare effectively for the new family that is soon to be created.

7

The Challenge of Teen Parenthood

At the health clinic of a large urban hospital, patients sit crowded together in a small, noisy reception room waiting to see a doctor. Laura W. is a social worker at the hospital where she runs a special program for teenage girls who come there during and after their pregnancies.

> *I am a single parent and [I know] that you have to get up every morning and try. You have to try harder. The tendency is to wake up in the morning with the word "can't." How am I going to get the baby to school and myself to school? How am I going to get my child to day care and me to work? You wake up with the word "can't" and you erase it. You get yourself going.*[1]

Feeling exhausted and overwhelmed by life is a common complaint among single parents whether they're divorced, widowed, or single teenagers who have never married. As the only parent, you're expected to do everything. This burden is especially difficult for teenagers because they are usually so unprepared for parenthood.

Since the overwhelming majority of single adolescent parents live at home with their own parents, they can generally rely on Mom and Dad for some support.[2] As you may recall from an earlier chapter, Helen's mother got up at night with her baby and handled some of the baby-sitting chores while Helen went off to school. Mothers can also teach their daughters the skills of proper child care, help them develop patience with an infant, and enable them to feel comfortable in a mothering role.

But there is a danger here, especially if Mom becomes too involved. In her book *School-Age Parents: The Challenge of Three-Generation Living*, Jeanne Warren Lindsay writes:

> *A comment I've heard often from teenage mothers is "I needed my Mom. She was too bossy, but I did need her. However, I wish she could have sometimes asked me instead of telling me what to do."*[3]

When it comes to raising a baby, parents often think that they know best and they may even try to take over all the responsibilities of child rearing themselves. During those early weeks and months when a close bond should be developing between a mother and child, the baby may instead be bonding with Grandma. Parents need to walk a thin line—offering to help their daughters, but not trying to take control from them. Even in the best of circumstances, however, conflicts can easily develop between a mother and daughter over what seems right for a child as he grows through infancy and into toddlerhood. Like anyone else learning to do something for the first time, a teenage mother feels unsure of herself and overly sensitive to criticism. Her mother, on the other hand, may be afraid that she will make mistakes that could harm the baby, or neglect him because she takes her responsibilities too lightly.

The best way of dealing with any misunderstandings and conflicts, experts say, is effective communication between an adolescent and her parents during the pregnancy and after the child's birth. First, everyone must recognize that the adolescent is the baby's parent, and therefore, his primary care-giver. Second, parents and children should be able to agree to disagree over different styles of parenting, and maintain their sense of humor. Third, an adolescent and her parents should work out a system of sharing responsibilities for child care that doesn't leave any one of them feeling overburdened or resentful.

THE ROLES OF A TEENAGE MOTHER

An adolescent mother is often expected to play many roles—student, employee, parent, adult, and teenager. It's too much too fast, and sometimes all of it can become overwhelming. Parents, of course, can help by caring for a child on a Saturday evening, for example, so their daughter can go out with her friends. This gives her the opportunity to be a teenager for awhile and set aside the duties of motherhood. Some parents even agree to care for a child during the day so their daughters can attend school. While sharing parenthood responsibilities can work very effectively, it may also lead to conflicts, especially if a mother begins to believe that her daughter is asking too much from her.

Fifty percent of all teenagers who give birth to a child before they reach the age of eighteen never finish high school.[4] This only increases the chances that they will be unable to find jobs and will be forced to accept welfare and live in poverty. Many of these girls were doing poorly in school before they became pregnant, so they have little motivation to return. Others may be unable to make child-care arrangements because their parents are working or simply aren't interested in caring for their children. As a result, they cannot attend school.

To deal with this problem, some schools across the country are providing special programs for teenage mothers which include day care for their children. At Rindge and Latin School in Cambridge, Massachusetts, for example, girls attend school during the day after leaving their children at an on-site nursery. In addition to their regular classes, the girls take courses in child development. They are also paired with mentors, successful adults in the community who may have been single adolescent mothers themselves. Since some of the girls receive welfare, they are taught how to make their way through the system so they can receive financial support. As a result of the Rindge and Latin program, almost ninety percent of the seniors graduated from high school.[5]

Other effective programs have been undertaken by the New Futures School in Albuquerque, New Mexico, and the Florence Crittendon School in Denver, Colorado. These programs are run in facilities that are separate from the regular high school. They appeal to some girls who prefer to be with other teenage mothers instead of going to classes with their peers who have not experienced a pregnancy. The girls begin attending the school during their pregnancy and continue after the birth of their children up until the time they graduate. In addition to the core academic curriculum, girls take courses in prenatal care and parenting while their children attend an on-site day-care facility.[6]

A key issue that's emphasized again and again in many of these programs is birth control. Today, at least one-third of the young girls who have a first pregnancy before age eighteen become pregnant again while they are still teenagers.[7] Girls with more than one child are far more likely to drop out of school and end up on welfare. The burden of multiple children is simply too great for most girls to handle and still attend high school classes regularly.

Some cities, like Denver, have even initiated programs to pay teenagers not to have a second pregnancy. Adolescents participating in a support group received one dollar for each day they did not become pregnant. This $365 per year is far lower than the $18,000 annually which the state estimates it spends on each pregnant teenager. The majority of these girls in the program did not become pregnant again, although they admitted that the primary reason was the peer pressure from other members of the support group, not the money.[8]

Many programs have been initiated at hospitals or medical centers which provide a combination of services for teenage mothers. They teach parenting skills, help the mothers find baby-sitting arrangements, build peer support to avoid a second pregnancy and help the girls build their self-esteem. As Laura W. explains, the girls "have very low self-esteem. They come from very low socio-economically depressed backgrounds. Their parents are not available to them in large part. Some of them are out of school already, or just about to quit school, so here they are about to have a baby."[9]

Few such programs exist. For example, there are only about 300 schools in forty-six states with programs to help teenage mothers.[10] Programs like these are still controversial because some critics fear they promote pregnancy. But there is no evidence to support this position. As Jeanne Lindsay explains: "Providing child care within the school system is perhaps the most important factor in making it possible for single-parent families to become self-sufficient."[11]

Other experts agree. In his book *The Teenage Parent's Child Support Guide*, Barry Schnell adds:

> Good child care is healthy for the young mother and her child. The teen mother is less isolated and can continue her education with her friends. It reduces many of the pressures of teen parenting and lessens the potential for child abuse. Being a teen parent does not have to be "a one-way ticket to poverty."[12]

WHAT HAPPENS TO THE FATHERS?

The girls in a teenage mothers' support program were asked to evaluate the fathers of their children on a scale from +10 to −10. Most rated the fathers with negative numbers because they had drifted away after the pregnancy occurred and refused to take any responsibility for their children. This is the stereotype of teen fathers—silent partners who abandon their girlfriends because they are too immature or too frightened to become parents. But, like all stereotypes, it only applies to some boys, not to all of them.

Manual Cardonna runs the Teen Fatherhood Project in Bridgeport, Connecticut, which he co-founded in 1983. Since that time, he has worked with over three hundred boys. The most difficult challenge, Cardonna says, is gaining their trust. So he goes out into the community to the hangouts of these young males—community centers, pool halls, bars, and street corners—and recruits them into the program. Why do these boys—some as young as thirteen—become fathers? Cardonna explains:

> It's the pressure. Sometimes it's the pressure from the girl to become pregnant. Sometimes it's the pressure from the boy's friends. Also, he is having problems at home. She is having problems at home. And they want to get out. This is the way to do it.[13]

Most of the boys in the program live with their girlfriends and their children. The program teaches these fathers parenting skills, helps them finish high school, and find jobs. The boys work in restaurants, factories, department stores, or construction. Cardonna was a teenage father himself but he still received a high school diploma and graduated from college. "I'm doing my best for these guys," he says, "because I was in this boat and I want to help them."

Cardonna often goes to a couple's home and provides counseling for them. He also helps them obtain medical care, deal with the welfare system and find housing assistance if they need it. "The best way to handle a pregnancy is to face it," he explains, "face up to your responsibility."[14]

THE EFFECTS OF TEENAGE PREGNANCY

Perhaps a partial answer to the long-term impact of teenage pregnancy has been provided by Frank Furstenberg and his associates, who studied approximately four hundred young mothers, the majority of them black, living in Baltimore over a period spanning the mid-1960s to the mid-1980s. As Furstenberg explains in his book *Adolescent Mothers in Later Life*, social scientists have long believed that teenage mothers usually drop out of school, generally live on welfare, are more likely to neglect or even abuse their children, who then grow up poor and repeat the pattern of their parents. But Furstenberg's study—the first to follow any teenage mothers for so many years—revealed some surprising results.

- Although many teenagers dropped out of high school after becoming pregnant, more than two-thirds eventually received their diplomas, and one-third even continued their education beyond secondary school.
- Only about one-quarter of the women were long-term welfare recipients. Most of the teenagers were working within two years after the birth of their child, having no desire to receive welfare which they found humiliating. The majority of women worked at low-paying jobs which created a struggle for them to provide enough for their families.

- In the 1960s, the majority of girls who became pregnant married, and the Baltimore women were no exception. But ten years later more than one-half of these marriages had ended in divorce. Some women married for a second time, and a few for a third time, while others remained single and may have lived with male friends.
- Interviews revealed that most of the young mothers did not neglect their children and attempted to provide them with adequate child care—often with parents or relatives—while they worked.
- Nevertheless, some of the children suffered because of their parents' circumstances. Furstenberg found that children were less prepared for school if their mothers were on welfare, if they had given birth to another child, and if they were unmarried. Presumably these mothers had less time to spend with a child and could provide a less secure home environment than other parents.
- By adolescence a much larger proportion of children were suffering problems. Half of the adolescents had repeated a grade or been suspended from school (compared to a fourth of the children born to women later in their lives). Teenagers whose mothers were on welfare, unmarried, and high school dropouts were far more likely to have failed a grade than other children.
- Approximately fifteen percent of the teenagers said they had been involved in a pregnancy (twenty-six percent of the girls and seven percent of the boys). This clearly shows that, contrary to popular belief, the majority of these

teenagers do not repeat the pattern of their parents. Nevertheless, a higher percentage of these teenagers becomes pregnant than those whose mothers were older when they gave birth to them. The children of teenage mothers also said that most of them knew they had been conceived while their mothers were still adolescents.

The results of Furstenberg's study indicate some definite long-term effects of teenage pregnancy, especially on adolescent children. As you may recall, a similar set of problems arose for the adolescent children of divorced parents. Furstenberg concludes:

> *The mothers' struggles to avoid poverty may have levied a cost on their children . . . The amount of time the teenage mother had available for care giving, the need for complex child-care arrangements, the absence of the father, lowered education . . . and, in some cases, reduced economic circumstances are all a familiar part of adolescent motherhood. Even with the help of family and friends, these obstacles were not, [and probably could not] be totally overcome.*[15]

PART FOUR

DEATH AND SINGLE-PARENT FAMILIES

8
Close-up:
A Death in the Family

As the holiday lights twinkled from across the living room, Brenda Olmstead slumped into an old, overstuffed sofa—exhausted and alone. The loneliness was still the worst part of it, and Brenda wondered whether she would have to spend the rest of her life this way. Her husband, Steve, had died almost a year earlier—a man who jogged three miles every day, dying of a heart attack at thirty-seven. It still seemed incredible.

Brenda's thoughts drifted back to the morning of the funeral, as she recalled standing in front of Steve's casket on that blustery February day with eleven-year-old Chris beside her. After the brief service had been concluded at the grave site and some of the mourners had already begun heading for the warmth of their cars, Brenda had placed a single rose on top of the coffin. At almost the same

Note: The story in this chapter is fictional, and the people are composites developed from interviews and research.

moment, Chris leaned forward and put something small and white beside it—the rabbit's foot his father had given him, just like the one Steve always carried. Then they turned and slowly walked away.

Over the next few weeks, Brenda became a whirlwind of activity. First, there were all the details to handle—applying for Steve's life insurance benefits, putting the house and joint bank accounts in her name, writing thank-you notes to all the people who had brought food on the day of the funeral, selecting a headstone for the gravesite, and paying the remaining bills. Fortunately, Steve had left enough money so she wouldn't have to move, but Brenda still needed her job to make ends meet financially. In the days following Steve's death, that job had seemed like her salvation. Since her mother had agreed to stay on after the funeral to help with Chris—and baby Jennifer, who was only six months old—Brenda found herself spending longer and longer hours at the office.

"It will be good for you," one of the other customer service supervisors had assured her. "It takes your mind off things."

Almost too late, Brenda discovered what a mistake she had made. One afternoon she was on an important conference call with several of the firm's West Coast sales representatives, when her eye caught the picture of Steve which always sat on the corner of her desk. Suddenly Brenda could feel the waves of emotion begin to build up inside her. Somehow, she was able to think of an excuse to cut short the conference call, before she was wracked with uncontrollable sobs. All the sadness which Brenda had refused to feel since the funeral had finally broken through.

During the time she was concentrating on work, Brenda had failed to pay enough attention to Chris, who was bravely engaged in his own lonely struggle to cope with his father's death. Chris kept his feelings inside, the way Brenda did, so she just assumed that he was recovering smoothly. His grandmother reported that Chris helped her make dinner and take care of Jennifer. At mealtime, he sat in his father's chair, and Brenda even saw him one afternoon playing with Steve's tennis racket. Clearly, Chris wanted to become the man of the house, just like his father.

Sitting alone on that first Christmas Eve following Steve's death, Brenda recalled how surprised she had been to discover that she and Chris had been going through almost the same grieving process. First there had been the shock of Steve's dying so suddenly, then the numbness when neither of them could or would feel anything. The numbness had ended for Brenda that day in her office. And one Saturday morning shortly afterward, she found herself sitting in front of the television looking at some of the videotapes she had made of their past holidays and vacations together. As pictures of Steve flashed onto the screen, the memories came flooding back and Brenda could feel her eyes fill with tears again. Suddenly, she felt a small hand on her shoulder and she looked up to see Chris, who was crying, too.

"I miss him so much," Chris said.

"I know," Brenda told him. "And we've both been too afraid to show it."

Steve had been Chris's idol. He wanted to play tennis as well as his father and learn to fish the way he did. When Chris graduated from elementary school in June, he sorely wished his dad could have been there to see him win the award for the school's most improved athlete. Afterward, Brenda took Chris to his favorite restaurant for a celebration, but it just wasn't the same for either of them without Steve.

Brenda had tried to be both mother and father to Chris, while also taking care of Jennifer and holding down a full-time job. Although she knew women who had become single parents after their divorce, Brenda had never realized how exhausting all the responsibilities could be. After her mother had left to return home and resume her numerous volunteer activities, Brenda was completely alone with no other adult to rely on for support.

Mornings and evenings were the most difficult times. While Chris was now old enough to get himself ready for school, there was still Jennifer to be fed, and dressed and dropped off each day at the day-care center. Steve had usually handled that task on his way to the university and even picked her up in the afternoon. He had also arranged to be at home most days when Chris arrived from school. Now he was one of those latchkey kids—a term Brenda had always hated—but there was nothing she could do about it.

Why did Steve have to die and leave her, she thought? Where was he when she really needed him? Other couples didn't have to go through this experience. Why was she so unlucky?

Evenings were often the most difficult. After putting dinner on the table, doing a load of laundry, and seeing the kids off to bed, Brenda was often so exhausted she could barely do anything except sit and stare into space. Then her loneliness was at its worst, and she longed to see Steve again.

In fact, during the several months immediately after he died, Brenda thought she had seen him—once at the supermarket when she had been shopping with Chris and Jennifer and again when they were together at the mall. Before he died, Steve had recorded a message on their answering machine which Brenda hadn't changed. While some of her friends thought it was strange to call and hear his voice, it was one of the ways for Brenda to hold onto him.

Brenda's longing for Steve and the emptiness she felt without him were supposed to diminish as the year went by—or, at least, that's the way some of her relatives and friends at the funeral had explained it. But her grief only seemed to grow deeper. At work she often described herself as having the attention span of a mosquito because her mind so easily drifted off to thoughts of Steve or Chris or Jennifer. And at the end of the day when she finally saw Jennifer—the child that she had conceived with Steve shortly before his death and whom he would never know—Brenda often found herself beginning to cry as she hugged and kissed her. She also wanted to spend more time with Chris and blamed herself for neglecting him.

What eventually helped Brenda out of this terrible depression were several close friends. One couple became like second parents to Chris and often took him camping along with their own three sons. In fact all of them were planning to come over and eat turkey dinner with Brenda and her children on Christmas Day. Another friend persuaded Brenda to join a single parents' support group which turned out to be a lifesaver. While most of the women were divorced, one was a young widow who could relate easily to Brenda's experiences. Gradually she came to terms with her grief and her anger. She began to value the time by herself not as loneliness but as aloneness from which she could draw strength. And she slowly started to recognize that she could function effectively on her own.

As Brenda looked back from the perspective of her first Christmas as a single parent, it was with the realization that she had finally begun living again. Oh, the pain and longing were still there— just as they surely were for Chris—but the future somehow seemed more assured.

9

Dealing with Death

"I was numb," one widow recalled, "and I went through a lot of things just very automatically because I knew they had to be done."[1] Another widow said:

> You feel like you've been removed from your body. You're some place else and you're just sort of viewing this whole scene without being able to comprehend the reality of it.[2]

The death of a beloved husband and father is so difficult to accept that many people at first refuse to accept it. In those terrible hours and days immediately following the death of a loved one, a numbness may settle over his survivors as they try to anesthetize themselves to the horrible reality of their loss. This is how they cope, at least at the beginning, with the awful shock of death. To the people around her, a woman may seem to be holding up bravely as she arranges her husband's funeral and stands with her children in front of the grave site at the cemetery. But many women report later that they were actually feeling nothing and have very little recollection of any of these events. They were too numb to feel and did everything "very automatically" and because "they had to be done."

Disbelief is how some people describe their immediate reaction to the death of a spouse or a parent. The entire experience seems like a nightmare from which they'll soon awake to see the loved one coming through the door again.

"I couldn't believe it," one man said, recalling his father's sudden death some years ago. "Dad had always been there for me, our whole family depended on him. He was our strength and now suddenly he wasn't there for us any more."[3]

For some, the death follows a long illness. One woman helped her husband battle a blood disorder that finally claimed his life after thirteen years. For others, death occurs more suddenly, from an unexpected heart attack, or an automobile accident, or in the case of one man, from the fiery crash of his single-engine plane. Sudden death may seem more shocking, but no matter what the circumstances, the awful finality of death is the same. The individual is gone, never to return to us, and nothing will ever be exactly as it was again.

HOW CHILDREN DEAL WITH DEATH

Experts agree that when a parent dies, children should usually be told as soon as possible so they can begin the process of coming to terms with death. A child's understanding is determined by his or her age and mental development. Preschool children, for example, believe that death is reversible and their dead parent will magically return to life. If Mommy has died, it is no different than if she had gone away on a long trip and eventually she will come back home again. Some well-meaning parents even make the mistake of explaining that the deceased has "gone away," leaving children with the mistaken belief that the dead person will suddenly reappear. In order to spare their children from the reality of death, parents may also tell them that dying is the same as sleeping. However, this often has the effect of making children afraid to go to sleep. Instead, a child needs to know the facts about death. A preschooler, for instance, may ask whether a parent breathes and eats and washes after death, imagining that it is a state very much like living. And these questions will need to be answered—not once, but over and over again— as a young child slowly tries to understand the meaning of death.

For older children, death raises different questions. Perhaps they've already experienced the death of a pet dog, so they know that death is irreversible and the body remains immobile. But they often seem to have a particular fascination in finding out about the grim details of what happens to the body as it lies underground. These children also recognize that if death can take one parent, it can claim the other parent, too. As one woman put it: "It's scary. The kids started asking what's going to happen if something happens to me." This anxiety is similar to the feelings that children experience following a divorce when one parent leaves and familiar family patterns are disrupted.

Children need particular reassurance that the remaining parent will probably not be taken from them, that life will go on, and that they will be secure.

In her book *Why Did Daddy Die?*, Linda Alderman explains that children may take longer than adults to express the profound grief that follows the death of a parent, because their first concern is with their own security.[4] But eventually the process of grieving begins and with it a wide range of conflicting emotions. A child may struggle with terrible feelings of guilt that her parent's death occurred because she was bad or in a fit of anger wished for the parent to die. Young children often believe that they possess magical powers to cause events just by wishing that they would occur. These same children may also experience anxiety at being separated from their remaining parent. A child who usually sleeps alone may crawl into bed with her mother at night, or cry upon leaving her mother for school the next morning. Children react to the death of a parent, as they do to divorce, by looking for extra security from the remaining parent. Sometimes a child grasps for security by regressing to an earlier age. A child who is toilet trained, for example, may begin wetting her diapers again. She returns to the behavior, the safety, of those days when she still had both parents.

Children also experience anger and profound sadness at a parent's death. One widow describes the feelings of two of her children who were in early and preadolescence when her husband died.

> *Laura was very angry . . . angry that he died. It wasn't fair, it wasn't appropriate. You're not supposed to do things like that. [My son] a very sensitive kind of kid was just profoundly sad. And I think if you strike the right chord with him on the right day you will sense that in the way he reacts to other people when it comes to*

the issue of death. . . . I have [a] friend whose mom was dying of cancer and she came over because she wanted to go to Ohio to visit her and she didn't know whether to take her two young children . . . because her mother wasn't looking too good at that point. And one thing I always did because [my husband's] illness was so serious was that I always involved the children when he had dialysis. After school, I would take [my son] over to the hospital . . . . And he was able to say to my friend, "You really should bring the children to see your mother because they should be able to say goodbye to her, too." And she said, "But you know she looks so awful now." And he said, "They'll remember how awful she looks for the next couple of months, but then they'll remember her when she played card games with them and walked in the park with them because that's the way I remember my dad now."[5]

Experts agree that children should be involved, as much as possible, with the process of death. If a parent suffers from a long illness, as this boy's father did, it is important for a child to understand the reality of the situation. This will later help the child accept death and work through his or her grief. For a similar reason, parents are also encouraged to have their children—unless they are very young—attend the funeral service. This enables them to cope with the finality of death and understand where the deceased has gone.

As children deal with their grief during the days and weeks following the funeral, they sorely need the empathy and support of their parents as well as other family members. In his book *How Do We Tell the Children?*, Dan Schaefer writes:

> *The way in which children work through their grief depends a lot on how their parents and the other members of their family handle themselves and whether or not . . . [they] reach out to them. The stronger the state of the helping adult, the better for the child. If the adult encourages the child to grieve, lets him know how much the dead person loved him and what joy the child brought to him, the youngster will be better able to cope.*[6]

A PARENT'S GRIEF

At the very time when children are most desperate for the help of their parents, they may be least capable of reaching out because they are themselves so overwhelmed with their own sense of loss. In her book *Lifelines*, Lynn Caine explains how afraid she was to be alone following her husband's death. She was lucky that her mother moved in and gave her a hand raising her two children because, Ms. Caine admits, she couldn't have done it herself. She felt completely drained trying to cope with the death of her husband and undertaking the responsibilities of single-parenthood.[7] Parents often have similar feelings following a divorce.

Once the numbness and the initial shock of a loved one's death wear off, the crushing reality hits. In *Seven Choices*, Elizabeth Harper Neeld explains that it took four days before she started crying over her husband's death and then she couldn't stop.[8] Neeld writes:

As every day passed, I realized more fully that I had not only lost a husband, I had lost the very purpose and shape of my life . . . I had no expectations. I had no plans.[9]

Men and women often talk about living only in the present because they cannot contemplate the future without their spouses. Author Rae Lindsay recalls bursting into tears in a restaurant, or a supermarket, or at family gatherings. She was also jealous of other couples who had each other when she felt so alone.[10] Many widows and widowers become angry at their dead spouses for leaving them, although they may recognize that these feelings are often totally irrational. But they are so upset that the dead person is no longer there to give them advice, or help with the children, or provide financial support, or love them any longer. As one widow put it: "Robert was my best friend and I didn't have him to consult with and I miss it."[11] Another woman confessed to being angry because she had been working on an important business deal in the days just before her husband succumbed to a brief illness that claimed his life. She realized that they could have enjoyed a few extra precious days together if she had not been so busy.

It's quite natural for adults to feel guilty following the death of a loved one, to ask themselves whether they might have done something to prevent the tragedy. Neeld's husband died of a heart attack while he was jogging, and she wondered whether there had been some physical signs of his heart condition beforehand that she had failed to notice.[12] After their spouses die, some people imagine seeing them, as Brenda did in the preceding chapter. This is a form of denial that may continue long after the initial shock and disbelief at a spouse's death have worn off. Somehow we still hope the nightmare will end, even though we know that the deceased can never return to us.

COPING WITH LIFE

In the weeks following the death of a spouse, when grief threatens to overwhelm them, single parents must somehow find the strength to deal with a myriad of important issues. Generally, the deceased leaves a will, which must be processed by an attorney. If there was any life insurance, the single parent must file a claim for it because the money is likely to provide critical financial support in the months ahead. In addition, children under eighteen are entitled to social security, and a spouse may also collect a monthly check if he or she earns less than a certain amount of money. But for the payments to begin, all the necessary forms must be filled out as soon as possible. There may also be joint bank accounts that have to be transferred to the name of the surviving spouse as well as a car or house that was owned jointly. If the parent had an illness preceding death, there are probably hospital bills that still have to be settled, and, of course, there are always funeral expenses that must be paid. One man who died suddenly, left behind a successful dental practice. His wife had to meet repeatedly with accountants and attorneys to pore through all of her husband's records, determine the value of the practice, and find someone to purchase it—a task which took weeks to complete.

In the aftermath of death, it's easy for the surviving parent to feel overburdened by all the problems that must be confronted. "I don't think I could have survived without the friends I had," explained the widow whose husband died suddenly, "the friends that became better friends throughout the whole thing."[13]

In our society, the two-parent family often seems to stand on its own, self-contained and self-reliant, a tiny, tight knit group of people who rely primarily on each other and no one else. But when one parent is suddenly removed, the remaining parent must begin looking elsewhere for support. "I'm very bad about asking for help," one widow confessed, "but I've learned, and I've learned that you get it . . . I like to give rather than being the one getting, but there are times when it just doesn't work."[14]

Single parents are required to carry out all the responsibilities that were formerly shared by two parents, and it's usually far too much to handle alone. As a widow explained:

> I'm awake half the night thinking about and putting into order the things that we should be doing the next day, between the yard work and maintenance around the house . . . working and child care and all the little things. One day I said, "You know every time I go into the bathroom the toilet paper thing is empty . . . when there were two adults in the house, there are two people doing that . . . When there's one person, it's only one person."[15]

Single parents—whether widowed or divorced—often find that out of necessity they must expand their families and look to other people for the type of assistance that used to be provided by their spouse. One widow talked about finding someone who knew about gardening to give her advice in this area, and someone else to help her invest the money from her husband's estate. "And so you pick up twenty people that you really didn't interact with before to fill in these gaps in your life," she explained.[16]

Parents and other relatives can help, too. They can play a critical role as surrogate parents. "Children need that extra hug," a widow said, "which only two parents have time enough to provide."[17] So children turn to other adults who, while they cannot replace a deceased parent, can give them some extra affection when they need it. A little girl crawls into the lap of her grandmother; a little boy grasps the hand of his friend's father on a trip to the zoo. Children reach out, just as their parents do, for love and support outside their immediate families.

These adults also serve as essential role models that children need for healthy development. In her book *Lifelines*, Lynn Caine explains that after her husband died, her thirteen-year-old son eventually started hanging out with a group of boys who were using drugs. When she found out and asked him for an explanation, he told her: "It's hard for me. I need a good male model."[18] Children who have lost a parent through death are often lacking this model. But sometimes a close family friend, a grandparent or other relative, can help fill in for the deceased parent.

It's an old cliché that "time is a great healer." And as the weeks and months go by, children gradually seem to adjust to the death of a parent. Sometimes they seem to take two steps forward and one step backward, like the little girl who was asked for her parents' names and addresses when she registered for the school band and spoke as if her father were still alive after he had been dead for a number of weeks. Children cope with death according to their own timetable.

During this period, children must be encouraged to express their feelings openly. If young people don't work through feelings of grief, abandonment, anger, and insecurity, these can affect their self-esteem and their ability to eventually form intimate relationships.[19] A young woman who has lost her father, for example, may be afraid of becoming too close to another man for fear he will be taken away. This is similar to the reaction that many girls have to a divorce.

Children need to remember their parents by looking at photographs or videotapes, to recall the good times they enjoyed together, and to share their feelings now that the parent is no longer with them. "We talk about him all the time," a widow said, referring to her deceased husband.[20]

Together parents and children must try to cope with the death of a loved one and gradually let go of the deceased until he or she becomes part of the past. In her book *Seven Choices*, Elizabeth Harper Neeld talks about the need to step back, put life into perspective, and begin to move forward. In her own case, she had to say to herself:

I will live through this loss. I will contribute to my own rehabilitation. I will incorporate this loss into my life and will move into the future. I will make the necessary changes.[21]

For some women these changes begin when they remove their husband's clothing and give it away, which symbolizes an important step in letting go of the past. Eventually single parents begin to set new goals for themselves. A widower decides to take a painting class; a widow enrolls in a program to become a physician's assistant and start a new career. Instead of barely surviving day to day—too tired or overcome with grief to think about the future—widows and widowers start living again. As a widow explained:

It took months to get to the point where I felt that I had two feet on the ground at last. And then it really wasn't until a year had gone by . . . that I could feel that we were crossing that boundary between the past life and starting to make a new life. All of a sudden one day, I said, "I don't think I thought about death today."[22]

But these changes do not occur without conflicts. As Neeld explains, individuals are afraid of forgetting about the deceased, and being disloyal to them if they move forward with their lives. They feel anxious about becoming involved in new activities, fearful of making mistakes and looking foolish. The alternative, however, is remaining stuck in the past.

Perhaps the most difficult issue facing many widows and widowers is whether to begin a new relationship. Unlike divorced parents, who generally dislike their former spouses, men and women who lose their spouse to death often idealize them, even if they were not always perfect. As a result, they may regard another relationship, at least at first, like a betrayal of the deceased, or may feel too overcome with sadness to consider going out with anyone. Society also expects widows and widowers to wait an appropriate length of time before they begin dating someone else—anything less is seen as dishonoring the dead. What's more, when single parents actually do begin dating, they often have the unavoidable habit of comparing everyone they meet with their deceased spouse— and usually the comparison is unfavorable. Until a single parent can move beyond the past, any satisfying long-term relationship will be impossible— the deceased will always intrude.

One widow explained that she tried to guard against making comparisons. And the man she was presently dating was actually superior to her deceased husband in some ways. When asked how her children responded to him, she explained:

> I don't think anyone ever replaces a father. I think someone else can replace a spouse . . . But kids will always have that sad part of the missing father. And it wouldn't matter who comes in, [he] might be someone that the kids end up liking and loving very much. But I think my kids are old enough and they have enough memories so that he'll never be their father.[23]

PART FIVE

SINGLE-PARENT FAMILIES— A COMMON THREAD

10

Single-Parent Families: Similar Challenges, Similar Needs

In single-parent families, one adult is expected to accomplish what two parents usually do in a more conventional family structure. It's no wonder, then, that single parents often feel stretched to the limit, and beyond, as they try to juggle the competing demands of home, work, school, and family while still trying to arrange a social life and maintain close friendships. It's a schedule that could exhaust anyone, and single parents are no exception.

For the recently divorced, the newly widowed, or the shy teenager who has just given birth to a baby, the first year of single parenthood is especially difficult. She or he must not only adjust to an unfamiliar, often confusing situation, but also deal with overpowering emotions that may run the gamut from intense sorrow to guilt, fear, loneliness, and extreme anger. Single parents sometimes talk about living in the present, at least at first, because the future seems far too uncertain and far too threatening to contemplate. A pregnant teenager who is abandoned by her boyfriend, a woman whose husband dies suddenly of a heart attack, a man whose wife walks out on him—all of them wonder: "How will I survive?"

But most single parents do survive. They gradually figure out what they can handle on their own and then learn to lean on others for the things they can't handle. Unlike the typical two-parent family, which tends to be more self-contained, single parents reach out, because they must, to grasp the hands of neighbors, friends, and relatives. Grandma baby-sits for her new grandson so her teenage daughter can go back to school. A widow finds people to help her unlock the mysteries of gardening and investing—two things her husband used to handle before his death.

As time goes by, many single parents begin to adjust to their new life-style and some even to flourish in it. In this book, one woman talked about the sense of relief she had experienced after finally being divorced from her husband, who was a compulsive gambler, and how she had gained confidence and learned to count on herself by becoming a successful single parent. A divorced dad spoke about the freedom he felt from making decisions on his own without consulting his ex-wife. And a widow explained that after a year had passed since her husband died, she finally went through an entire day without thinking about death. This was a turning point for her, a clear indication that she was finally ready to move forward with her life.

For other single parents, however, the transition takes far longer, and may never really occur at all. In her studies of divorced couples, Dr. Judith Wallerstein found that young women often recovered more rapidly than older women. Since they had been married longer, these women mourned the loss of their role as wives far more deeply, and frequently faced a very dim prospect of developing new intimate relationships. What's more, they may have left the workplace many years earlier to raise their children, so the chances of them finding an adequate job were very slim.

Money is one of the most critical issues facing single parents. Since most of them are women, they traditionally earn much less than men. To make matters worse, at least thirty percent of divorced husbands fail to pay court-ordered child support. Many widows are left with inadequate income by their deceased husbands. And most teenage mothers earn little or nothing—they must depend on their parents or on welfare for support. Consequently, a high number of single-parent families are forced to struggle financially, with many living near or below the poverty line and some even forced to join the ranks of the homeless. This is enough to produce enormous strains on the fabric of any family.

CHILDREN

Perhaps the question most often asked about single-parent families is this: "How well are the children raised?" Earlier in the book, one boy explained that his dad was both a mother and father to him. A single mom said that raising her daughter had become "my mission in life," and she was trying to provide her with all of the security, stability, and love she needed. There is no question that many single parents raise happy, psychologically healthy children. But there is also little doubt that one parent often cannot do everything that two parents do—and single parents realize this fact. As a result they often must turn to adults outside the immediate family to fill in as surrogate parents.

Single parents also recognize that their children may be struggling with tough problems that arise from the creation of their single-family structure. A little boy whose mother has died experiences intense sadness, and fears that his other parent may somehow be taken from him. A girl whose parents have divorced, lives through a long, unpleasant conflict between her parents leading up to a nasty break up which involves a bitter court battle. This type of experience leaves scars that take a long time to heal. The child may be struggling with feelings of guilt, believing that somehow she caused the divorce, deep sadness over the loss of her two-parent family, as well as intense anger at both her parents for not making the marriage work. The child also must begin to develop a different kind of relationship with the out-of-home parent, usually the father, and this may be extremely difficult. Unfortunately, many men drift away from their children following a divorce and an estimated forty percent of them rarely, if ever, see their fathers.

As the divorce recedes into the past, its impact on children begins to diminish and they adjust to their new families. Nevertheless, Dr. Judith Wallerstein has discovered that some serious long-standing effects may still remain. Young women, for example, may hesitate to form intimate relationships, fearing that they will be unsuccessful just like their parent's marriage. Adolescent boys, whose fathers have left them, may lack the role model they need to then form a firm sense of male identity. Additionally, these boys may not have the proper motivation to succeed in school or embark upon successful careers.

Similar problems have surfaced in the studies of children raised by single teenage parents. While the majority provide their children with proper care, this may not be sufficient to prevent a significant number of them from encountering serious difficulties during adolescence. These include failing grades in school and becoming adolescent parents just as their mothers did.

PROSPECTS FOR THE FUTURE

The single-parent family is here to stay—in fact, its ranks have been growing as a result of a rising divorce rate and an increasing number of teenage girls giving birth to children. With approximately ten million of these families in our society, they present us with several important issues that are not yet being properly addressed.

An alarmingly high percentage of teenage girls, for example, do not receive adequate medical care throughout their pregnancy. In part, this is because they may try to deny the pregnancy to themselves during the early months and, therefore, fail to see a doctor as soon as possible. In some rural and urban areas, however, good, low-cost health care is simply unavailable to the poor so pregnant teens may not receive complete medical examinations, regular checkups or the proper advice on how to maintain a healthy diet throughout their pregnancy.

After they give birth, an estimated fifty percent of all teenage girls never return to high school, which severely limits their opportunities to find decent jobs. For some, the reason is simply lack of motivation. But many girls are prevented from returning because they cannot find adequate day care for their children. While some high schools provide on-site day care, the vast majority do not. Nor do towns and cities have enough low-cost day care to meet the needs of the parents who need it. Some communities seem reluctant to offer on-site day care at local high schools because of the cost or the popular belief that it may encourage young girls to become pregnant and have children. Although there are no studies to support this viewpoint, the net result for too many teenage mothers is that they are denied an education and an opportunity to eventually become self-supporting. Instead, they are often forced to resort to welfare, which is far more expensive than the price of adequate day-care facilities.

The need for high quality, easily affordable child care is perhaps the single most important problem facing single parents—whether they are teenagers, widows, or divorced moms and dads. Some companies have recognized this issue and now provide on-site day-care centers for the children of their employees. Others make arrangements with local facilities so employees can bring their children there at reduced rates. In addition, many corporations have initiated job-sharing programs, which enable employees to work part-time, as well as flexible hours that permit parents to accommodate their children's schedule more easily.

Nevertheless, these programs still must be greatly expanded.

In addition, children may need help dealing with divorce or the death of a parent. Some single parents are simply incapable of redirecting their own lives following the end of a marriage and dealing with the very immediate concerns of a child who is also experiencing a tremendous upheaval. While some schools and communities have developed programs for children who have lost a parent through death or divorce, a large number of children are still forced to deal with these problems on their own. Perhaps the proper guidance would enable more of them to work through their feelings successfully and avoid any serious long-term effect on their own relationships and their families in the future.

Source Notes

CHAPTER ONE

1. *Newsweek*, Winter/Spring 1990, p. 16.
2. Jeffrey Simpson, *The American Family: A History in Photographs* (New York: Viking, 1976), p. 11.
3. *Ibid.*, p. 33.
4. Steven Mintz and Susan Kelley, *Domestic Revolutions: A Social History of the American Family* (New York: The Free Press, 1988), p. 62.
5. *Ibid.*, p. 111.
6. *Ibid.*, p. 108.
7. Ralph Waldo Emerson, *Representative Men: Montaigne.*
8. *Newsweek*, Winter/Spring 1990, p. 16.
9. Mintz and Kelley, p. 109.
10. *Ibid.*, p. 161.
11. Betty Friedan, *The Feminine Mystique* (New York: W.W Norton, 1963), pp. 240, 255.
12. *Newsweek*, Winter/Spring 1990, p. 16.

13. Mintz and Kelley, p. 112.
14. *The World Almanac*, 1991 (New York: Pharos Books, 1990), p. 841.
15. Philip J. Hills, "Birth-Control Backlash," *The New York Times Magazine*, December 16, 1990, p. 7.
16. Felicity Barringer, "After Long Decline, Teen Births Are Up," *The New York Times*, August 17, 1990, Section A, p. A14.

CHAPTER TWO

1. Laurence Johnson, "The Children of Divorce," *The Single Parent*, March/April 1990, p. 6.
2. Geoffrey Greif and Alfred DeMaris, "Dads Raising Kids: A New Survey," *The Single Parent*, January/February, 1989, p. 12.

CHAPTER THREE

1. Interview with A.
2. Judith S. Wallerstein and Joan Berlin Kelly, *Surviving the Breakup* (New York: Basic Books, 1980), p. 11.
3. Interview with A.
4. Interview with B.
5. Interview with C.
6. National Public Radio, April 2, 1991.
7. Carol Lawson, "Schools Try to Help Children in Divorces." *The New York Times*, December 27, 1990, Section C, pp. 1, 9.
8. Jane Brody, "Children of Divorce: Steps to Help Can Hurt," *The New York Times*, July 23, 1991, Section C, p. 9.
9. Tamar Lewin, "New Tools for States Bolster

Collection of Child Support," *The New York Times*, June 15, 1991, pp. 1, 9.

10. Interview with A.
11. Sheila Weller, "One Woman's Family: The Plight of Single Mothers," *McCall's*, February, 1989, p. 76.
12. Steven Mintz and Susan Kellogg, *Domestic Revolutions: A Social History of American Family Life* (New York: The Free Press, 1988), p. 216.
13. John DeFran, Judy Fricke, Julie Elmen, *On Our Own* (Lexington, Mass: D.C. Heath, 1987), p. 21.
14. Charles Dervaries, "Single Parents and the Housing Crunch," *The Single Parent*, January/February, 1990, p. 7.
15. Interview with D.
16. Interview with A.
17. Interview with C.
18. Deane-Jo Moore, "A Parent, Not a Pal," *The Single Parent*, May/June 1990, pp. 16–17.
19. David Koulack, "Parent or Companion?" *The Single Parent*, July/August 1990, pp. 38–39.
20. Interview with A.
21. Interview with D.
22. Interview with A.
23. Weller, p. 80.

CHAPTER FOUR

1. Judith S. Wallerstein and Sandra Blakeslee, *Second Chances* (New York: Ticknor and Fields, 1989), p. 302.
2. *Ibid.*, pp. 214–215.
3. *Ibid.*, pp. 49–52.
4. Jane Brody, "Children of Divorce: Steps to Help Can Hurt," *The New York Times*, July 23, 1991, Section C, p. 1.

5. Interview with D.
6. Judith S. Wallerstein and Joan Berlin Kelly, *Surviving the Breakup* (New York: Basic Books, 1980), p. 207.
7. Interview with D.
8. *Surviving the Breakup*, p. 165.
9. Interview with C.
10. Sheila Weller, "One Woman's Family: The Plight of Single Mothers," *McCall's*, February 1989, p. 80.
11. Interview with A.
12. Second Chances, pp. 261–267.
13. Jill Krementz, *How It Feels When Parents Divorce* (New York: Knopf, 1987), pp. 54–55.

CHAPTER FIVE

1. Barbara Kantrowitz, "Breaking the Poverty Cycle," *Newsweek*, May 28, 1990, p. 78.
2. Felicity Barringer, "After Long Decline, Teen Births Are Up," *The New York Times*, August 17, 1990, Section A, p. A14.

CHAPTER SIX

1. Linda Brown, "Pregnant Teenagers Less Likely to Get Proper Medical Treatment," *Charlotte Observer*, November 27, 1984, p. C10.
2. Richard Prince, "Preventing Teen Pregnancy Is Still the Best Policy," *Fairpress*, January, 1991, p. 17.
3. Philip J. Hills, "Birth-Control Backlash," *The New York Times Magazine*, December 16, 1990, p. 70.
4. Barbara Kantrowitz, "Homeroom," *Newsweek*, Special Issue, Summer/Fall 1990, p. 54.

5. Leon Dash, *When Children Want Children* (New York: William Morrow, 1989), p. 12.
6. *Ibid.*, pp. 124, 207.
7. Elizabeth Culotta, "New Tactics Urged to Cut Teen Births," *Milwaukee Journal*, February 17, 1990.
8. Dash, p. 121.
9. Brown, p. C10.
10. *Ibid.*, p. C10.
11. Dash, p. 23.

CHAPTER SEVEN

1. Interview with E.
2. Barry T. Schnell, *The Teenage Parent's Child Support Guide* New York: (The Advocacy Center for Child Support, 1988), p. 76.
3. Jeanne Warren Lindsay, *School-Age Parents: The Challenge of Three-Generation Living* (Buena Park, Calif.: Morning Glory Press, 1990), p. 84.
4. Schnell, p. 27.
5. Barbara Kantrowitz, "Homeroom," *Newsweek*, Summer/Fall 1990, pp. 50–54.
6. *NEA Today*, March 1991, p. 6.
7. Lisbeth B. Schorr, *Within Our Reach* (New York: Anchor Press, 1988), p. 50.
8. Ann Zimmerman, "Buying Time for Teens," *Dallas Times Herald*, April 4, 1989, p. C11.
9. Interview with E.
10. Kantrowitz, pp. 50–54.
11. Lindsay, p. 153.
12. Schnell, p. 27.
13. Interview with Manual Cardonna.
14. *Ibid*.
15. Frank F. Furstenberg, J. Brooks-Gunn, and S. Philip Morgan, *Adolescent Mothers in Later Life*

(New York: Cambridge University Press, 1987), p. 104.

CHAPTER NINE

1. Interview with F.
2. Interview with G.
3. Interview with H.
4. Linda Alderman, *Why Did Daddy Die?* (New York: Pocket Books, 1989), p. 54.
5. Interview with F.
6. Dan Schaefer and Christine Lyons, *How Do We Tell the Children?* (New York: Newmarket Press, 1986), p. 45.
7. Lynn Caine, *Lifelines* (New York: Doubleday, 1978), pp. 14–24.
8. Elizabeth Harper Neeld, *Seven Choices* (New York: Clarkson N. Potter, 1990), p. 20.
9. *Ibid.*, p. 25.
10. Rae Lindsay, *Alone and Surviving* (New York: Walker and Company, 1972), pp. 36–39.
11. Interview with F.
12. Neeld, p. 22.
13. Interview with G.
14. Interview with F.
15. *Ibid.*
16. *Ibid.*
17. Interview with G.
18. Caine, p. 89.
19. Alderman, pp. 98–99.
20. Interview with G.
21. Neeld, p. 169.
22. Interview with F.
23. *Ibid.*

Bibliography

BOOKS

Alderman, Linda. *Why Did Daddy Die?* New York: Pocket Books, 1989.

Caine, Lynn. *Lifelines*. Garden City, N.Y.: Doubleday, 1978.

Dash, Leon. *When Children Want Children*. New York: William Morrow, 1989.

DeFran, John, Judy Fricke, and Julie Elmen. *On Our Own*. Lexington, Mass.: D.C. Heath, 1987.

Friedan, Betty. *The Feminine Mystique*. New York: Norton, 1963.

Furstenberg, Frank F., J. Brooks-Gunn, and S. Philip Morgan. *Adolescent Mothers in Later Life*. New York: Cambridge University Press, 1987.

Krementz, Jill. *How It Feels When Parents Divorce*. New York: Knopf, 1987.

Lindsay, Jeanne Warren. *School-Age Parents: The Challenge of Three-Generation Living*. Buena Park, Calif.: Morning Glory Press, 1990.

Lindsay, Rae. *Alone and Surviving*. New York: Walker and Company, 1972.

Mintz, Stephen and Susan Kellogg. *Domestic Revolutions: A Social History of the American Family.* New York: The Free Press, 1988.

Neeld, Elizabeth Harper. *Seven Choices.* New York: Clarkson N. Potter, 1990.

Schaefer, Dan and Christine Lyons. *How Do We Tell the Children?* New York: Newmarket Press, 1986.

Schnell, Barry T. *The Teenage Parent's Child Support Guide.* New York: The Advocacy Center for Child Support, 1988.

Schorr, Lisbeth B. *Within Our Reach.* New York: Anchor Press, 1988.

Simpson, Jeffrey. *The American Family: A History in Photographs.* New York: Viking, 1976.

Wallerstein, Judith S. and Sandra Blakeslee. *Second Chances.* New York: Ticknor and Fields, 1989.

Wallerstein, Judith S. and Joan Berlin Kelly. *Surviving the Breakup.* New York: Basic Books, 1980.

ARTICLES

Ball, Joanne. "A Narrow Gap of Generations." *Boston Globe,* August 11, 1987.

Barringer, Felicity. "After Long Decline, Teen Births Are Up." *New York Times,* August 17, 1990.

Brody, Jane. "Children of Divorce: Steps to Help Can Hurt." *New York Times,* July 23, 1991.

Brown, Linda. "Pregnant Teenagers Less Likely to Get Proper Medical Treatment." *Charlotte Observer,* November 27, 1984.

Culotta, Elizabeth. "New Tactics Urged to Cut Teen Births." *Milwaukee Journal,* February 17, 1990.

Dervaries, Charles. "Single Parents and the Housing Crunch." *The Single Parent*, January/February, 1990.

Greif, Geoffrey and Alfred Demaris. "Dads Raising Kids: A New Survey." *The Single Parent*, January/February 1989.

Hills, Philip J. "Birth-Control Backlash." *New York Times Magazine*, December 16, 1990.

Johnson, Laurence. "The Children of Divorce." *The Single Parent*, March/April 1990.

Kantrowitz, Barbara. "Breaking the Poverty Cycle." *Newsweek, 1990.*

————. *"Homeroom" Newsweek* Special Issue, Summer/Fall, 1990.

Koulack, David. "Parent or Companion?" *The Single Parent*, July/August, 1990.

Lawson, Carol. "Schools Try to Help Children in Divorces." *New York Times*, December 27, 1990.

Lewin, Tamar. "New Tools for States Bolster Collection of Child Support." *New York Times*, June 15, 1991.

Lewis, Donna. "Learning to Be Parents—And Not to Be." *Atlanta Journal*, March 25, 1990.

Marek, Elizabeth. "The Lives of Teenage Mothers." *Harper's Magazine*, April, 1989.

Moore, Deane-Jo. "A Parent, Not a Pal." *The Single Parent*, May/June, 1990.

Mullener, Elizabeth. "Teen Pregnancy Has Its Own Reasons, Experts Say." *New Orleans Times—Picayune*, February 17, 1990.

O'Crowley, Peggy. "Houses Divided." *Hackensack Record*, March 28, 1990.

Prince, Richard. "Preventing Teen Pregnancy Is Still the Best Policy." *Fairpress*, January, 1991.

Rea, Tom. "Conference Opens on Teen Pregnancy." *Casper Star Tribune*, December 6, 1988.

Rubin, Nancy. "America's New Homeless." *McCall's*, November, 1988.

Taylor, Paul. "Making Deadbeat Dads Pay Up." *Washington Post Weekly*, December 31, 1990.

Weller, Sheila. "One Woman's Family: The Plight of Single Mothers." *McCalls*, February, 1989.

Zimmerman, Ann. "Buying Time for Teens." *Dallas Times Herald*, April 4, 1989.

Index

About the Author

Richard Worth is a writer/producer of documentaries and corporate video presentations, as well as the author of eight books, including *The American Family*; *You'll Be Old Someday, Too*; *The Third World Today*; *Robert Mugabe of Zimbabwe*; and *Creating Corporate Audio-Visual Presentations*. He also has written an eight-part radio series on legendary New York City mayor Fiorello LaGuardia that aired on National Public Radio. He lives in Connecticut.